new style
for
old junk

julie **collins**

new style
for
old junk

CREATIVE AND CONTEMPORARY IDEAS
FOR TRANSFORMING JUNKSHOP FINDS

MURDOCH
BOOKS

This book is dedicated to my talented grandmother, Zilpah Louisa Clother,
who inspired me to be creative.

Love and appreciation to my mother Thelma Collins, whose help, support and
encouragement enabled me to work and complete this book. Also to my friends Peter
White, Jane Hutchinson and Mark Harris for their help.

First published 1996 by Merehurst Limited. Reprinted 2001.

Copyright © Murdoch Books UK Ltd 1996

ISBN 1 903992 05 2

A catalogue record for this book is available from the British Library.

Editor: **Geraldine Christy**
Designers: **Sue Rawkins and Anthony Cohen**
Artworks: **Brihton Illustration**
Stylist: **Clare Hunt**
Photographer: **Graeme Ainscough**
(with the expception of pages 28, 30, 75, 76, 77, 82 & 83:
photos courtesy of *Home Flair*, © Hamerville Magazines Limited)

CEO: **Robert Oerton**
Publisher: **Catie Ziller**
Production Manager: **Lucy Byrne**
International Sales Director: **Kevin Lagden**

Colour separation by Bright Arts, Hong Kong
Printed in Italy by Giunti Industrie Grafiche

Murdoch Books (UK) Ltd
Ferry House, 51–57 Lacy Road,
Putney, London, SW15 1PR, UK
Tel: +44 (0)20 8355 1480
Fax: +44 (0)20 8355 1499
Murdoch Books (UK) is a subsidiary
of Murdoch Magazines Pty Ltd.

UK Distribution
Macmillan Distribution Ltd
Houndsmills, Brunell Road
Basingstoke, Hampshire, RG1 6XS, UK
Tel: +44 (0) 1256 302 707
Fax: +44 (0) 1256 351 437
http://www.macmillan-mdl.co.uk

Murdoch Books®
GPO Box 1203
Sydney, NSW 1045, Australia
Tel: +61 (0)2 8220 2000
Fax: +61 (0)2 8220 2020
Murdoch Books® is a trademark
of Murdoch Magazines Pty Ltd

contents

introduction 6

sourcing **junk items** 8

developing an eye for a **bargain** 12

terms and techniques 16

LIVING ROOM

glass-fronted **cupboard** 28

painted **coffee table** 31

heraldic writing **desk** 33

granite effect **fireplace** 37

DINING ROOM

verdigris and crystal **chandelier** 39

display **decanter** and glasses 42

dinner **decanter and glasses** 45

transforming plain **wooden chairs** 46

Scandinavian style **scroll chair** 48

simple folk art style **chair** 51

Oriental lacquered **chair** 54

Shaker style **chair** 56

KITCHEN

vine leaf **table** 58

pine panelled **cupboard** 64

BATHROOM

shutters and **louvre doors** 68

bathroom **cupboard** 71

BEDROOM

wardrobe and **headboard** 74

folding filigree **screen** 79

gilt stencilled **mirror** 82

carved **linen cupboard** 84

CHILDREN'S ROOMS

cherub **wardrobe** 87

toy soldier **bedstead** 93

ACCESSORIES AND GIFTS

mosaic terracotta **vase** 96

calligraphy **lampshades** 98

malachite painted **box** 101

templates 106

suppliers 111

index 112

introduction

I inherited my love of dusty, crammed junk shops from my grandmother, and later from my mother. I can remember the excitement of queuing outside church halls waiting for jumble sales to start, clutching my pocket money and surging forward with the crowd when the doors opened. I always headed straight for the bric-a-brac counter where I found wonderful treasures, often hidden inside a box full of bits and pieces, for just a few pence. I bought wooden boxes, pictures, old toys and books, and on occasions unknowingly found really good antiques. There was even more excitement when we arrived home and reviewed all our bargains. I went through my finds, painstakingly cleaned and polished items and gave them pride of place on shelves in my bedroom. I never lost the thrill of buying bargains and as I grew older I went with my mother to junk shops on a regular basis, also taking in any car boot or jumble sales that were accessible.

Our house was always full of activity, and I was taught to sew, knit, crochet and paint from a young age, as my mother and grandmother were very creative with their hands and always encouraged us to learn their skills, while my father sketched and painted. I particularly remember sitting with my grandmother making angels from pieces of card, cutting out wings and coating them with glitter, then hand painting the faces. Grandmother went to numerous classes where she made soft furnishings, millinery, cane baskets and trays, pewter frames and leather gloves. During our school holidays my sister and I were also taken and we worked alongside her, making our own masterpieces. I developed a passion for creating things, and have never lost that thrill. My grandfather was a signwriter and grainer, and I remember watching as he transformed plain painted doors into maple, oak and a variety of other wood finishes, and was amazed when he dipped his thumb into oils and glazes and, with a simple twist, created a lifelike knot in the wood. His father was in the same profession and he was apprenticed to him in the Victorian era, when graining was very popular. I was privileged to have such a creative childhood, and make sure I put this valuable quality time into my own daughter's life.

When I acquired my first home the search in the junk shops was a much more serious affair as I had to be more practical and look for items I needed, but I often found myself coming home with something quite impractical that I knew I could transform into a designer piece. I knew I had passed my bargain hunting bug onto my small daughter when she recently asked a stall owner at a car boot sale if she could have an old wooden box for ten pence, with no prompting at all from me …

I had a successful career in show business, appearing in London West End theatres and on television. As I worked flexible hours and had resting periods, I decorated my own home, created different rooms for friends and relatives, and gradually learnt new techniques until I was able to create a really professional finish. Architects and interior designers who had seen my work began to offer me private commissions, and this grew into a small business that I was able to fit in between my professional show business bookings. Projects ranged from small houses to large restaurants, at home and abroad. I began to be expert in making curtains and covering furniture, gaining much of my tuition from books and heeding tips from other people.

Following the birth of my daughter, a friend arranged an interview for me with the editor of *Home Flair* interiors magazine, Dawn Leahey. She was very complimentary about my portfolio and gave me a step-by-step feature on making and decorating my large screen. At this time I had just purchased a Victorian ground floor flat in a dilapidated state, and I asked if the magazine would like to do step-by-step features on a total refurbishment of the flat, as I would be buying all the furniture, fixtures and fittings from junk shops, working within a very tight budget. Thus my junk shop series was born, culminating in the writing of this book.

During this time I was commissioned to paint the interior of a restaurant, and totally transformed 80 old church chairs, by rubbing down, fixing carved scrolled backs, hand painting designs and creating a crackled aged finish – techniques that I have demonstrated for you here in the projects.

I was very proud to be invited to the Albert Hall with a past business associate for a meeting to discuss the possibility of replicating the Victorian splendour stencil used in the original decorations of the staircases, which had been obscured by layers of paint over the years. I was taken to the cellars where I was able to trace parts of the stencilled design and painstakingly recreate a new stencil and apply the design to their satisfaction. We were commissioned to carry out this refurbishment on an entire staircase.

I have now come full circle as, having spent the last eleven years in interiors, I am now back doing television appearances, not as a performer but as an interior designer and specialist in painting junk furniture.

I hope that by sharing my success with you, and the fact that I have no formal art training, you will feel encouraged to experiment yourself and go from strength to strength in finding bargains, trying out the projects in the book and creating your own masterpieces.

sourcing
junk items

The most important points to look for when you are buying old furniture are the shape and the condition of the piece. It is still possible to find wonderful pieces of furniture that could sell in auctions at quite a high price, by searching in junk shops, street markets and car boot sales. I have also found beautiful doors, old mirrors and small items thrown into skips outside houses being refurbished, but it is wise to ask if you can take something away before you remove it. When large houses are being renovated some of the wonderful old fixtures and fittings are ripped out, and these can often be seen outside propped against the garden wall with a 'For Sale' notice displayed on them. This is how I recently acquired two large solid wood radiator covers, a large oval wooden-framed wall mirror, louvre doors, large picture frames, Lloyd Loom chairs and a cast-iron fireplace. You have to look often, be patient, learn to barter and examine pieces carefully to see how well they are made.

Junk shops

A good time to visit junk shops is at the weekends, as dealers are often engaged in house clearances at that time and, owing to lack of room in their shops, may be keen to sell the pieces quickly. Take time to poke about in the back of the shops, behind cupboards and in corners. Sometimes you may find something that you are not sure about, but look at the piece carefully; consider if it would suit your purpose and, if you like the overall look of it, think of improvements that you could make. Try to picture the finished product in your mind.

You will soon get to know which shops have good quality furniture and interesting pieces, and price them realistically. Once you are a regular customer dealers are usually happy to give you a good price and at times I have negotiated items in part exchange. Most shops will deliver free of charge if you live reasonably near. If you find several items in one shop they are often open to negotiation on a price for the lot; also a deposit may enable you to reserve an item. One point you must always keep in mind when visiting junk shops is that they have a lot of customers and a quick turnover of stock. I have often been furious with myself for not snapping up something on the spot, and when I have returned after thinking about it before deciding to buy, the item has been sold. 'He who hesitates is lost' must be your motto!

Newspaper advertisements

Look through the pages of local papers regularly to see if any house content sales are advertised. When people move house, they often have pieces of furniture or odds and ends that will not fit into their new home, or that they do not want to keep. It is a good idea to telephone to find out exactly what they are selling, or otherwise turn up early. Older people often move from a large family home into a bungalow, flat or much smaller house, so they may have a surplus of furniture, and I have found wonderful bargains in this way.

Sometimes I set off with a specific piece in mind that I wish to find, but other times I go with an open mind. I always look for smaller pieces that I can refurbish and make into gifts, such as small wooden boxes, picture frames, small mirrors, ceramic pieces, lampshades and bases and anything else that catches my eye.

Garage sales

Garage sales are advertised in local papers or sometimes on posters. Many people prefer to put everything in the garage or garden so that they do not have to invite strangers into their home or transport items to another venue. It also gives them the opportunity to show larger pieces that are for sale. I have been to many of these when the house owners are moving abroad and want to get rid of almost everything in their home. It is well worth searching through boxes of odd pieces for such objects as door handles and hinges that are being sold cheaply. These useful items might turn out to be just the thing you need, and help keep down the costs when needed for a project. I recently found a small box in such a sale, and when I opened it there were 12 new brass decorative small door knobs, still wrapped in paper, complete with all the screw fittings, at a fraction of the price I would have to pay in a shop. These are the sort of thing I use constantly, and you should always snap up such a bargain.

Car boot sales

Car boot sales have become very popular and there are regular venues where there are sometimes two or three hundred cars selling a variety of objects. This is the way many people choose to get rid of items they do not want, especially when they are moving house. Apart from useful bits and pieces, I have found amazing bargains such as decorative screens, small decorative chairs, fire screens, trunks, wooden boxes, lamps, light fittings and numerous other pieces. If I feel the price is too high for an item, I do try and knock them down, but usually they are very reasonable. It is a good idea to have a second walk around before the sale finishes, as often sellers do not want to take the items back home again and will sell them for a low price rather than have to do so.

I met an old couple recently at a car boot sale who had cleared out their garage and were selling its contents, and at first glance I saw nothing of interest to me. However, on looking more closely, I found a pile of pieces of wood, and when I went through it carefully, there were pieces of oak, pine and mahogany. These are useful if you have good, but damaged, pieces of furniture that need restoring. They are expensive to buy, so I snapped them up and have used several of them very effectively to turn a damaged item into a new-looking finished piece, with very little outlay. At the same sale I found another box containing old furnishing fringes and trims, wooden feet for furniture, four old brass castors and a decorative carved wood piece, all of which I am sure I will put to good use. At the end of another sale I looked through a box and noticed a large brass lion head door knocker. The man told me to take away the whole box for £1. When I got home I found it contained a complete set of good quality brass front door furniture, including a number ten. I was in the process of purchasing my new home, which was number ten. The box was obviously just waiting for me to collect it!

Auctions

Another good place to source junk furniture is at local auctions, and you will find these advertised in your local paper. Go and walk around on the viewing day and obtain a catalogue list, and carefully examine any pieces you might be interested in bidding for. You do not want to buy a piece that has dry rot or too much woodworm, or has been made from poor quality wood or badly repaired. Decide the price you want to pay and stick to it. If you are a novice at auctions do go two or three times to view only, to get the idea of how it is run, and how to make your bids; also this will give you a good idea of current prices. Auctions are conducted so fast that if you do not keep up with proceedings and have not carefully marked the piece you are interested in, you could end up buying something quite different. This reminds me of the story of my aunt, who bid at an auction for a large colour television and when she went to collect it after the sale found she had mixed up the lot numbers and had purchased a large old wringer. All was not lost, however, as her husband turned the base into a very solid garden table, using an old door on top – the talent of transformation obviously runs in the family.

Charity shops

Charity shops sell a variety of bric-a-brac, pottery, lampshades and other small items, as well as large pieces of furniture. Donations come in regularly, so stock changes constantly.

Church fittings dealers

There are specialized dealers all over the country who buy church furniture when it is no longer required. The dealers have large storage premises and vehicles, and organizations tend to get one person to come and clear the pews, vast quantities of chairs and on occasions pulpits, lecterns, windows, etc.

Let your imagination run free when looking at a piece – a plain light fitting can be turned into a simulated chandelier, a dirty carved wooden cupboard into a painted and decorated masterpiece, an old ceramic lamp completely transformed by painting and stencilling. Always keep on the lookout for remnants of old materials, such as tapestries, velvets and brocades to use for covering chair seats, stools and cushions.

developing
an eye for
a **bargain**

f you are not used to buying second-hand furniture, the first thing you need to do is visit plenty of second-hand shops and sales to get a good idea of the market prices. Attend a local auction, get a catalogue and make a note of the prices that are fetched. This gives you a general idea of current values. There are many professional dealers at auctions, who are looking to restore or retail again, so the prices they give are usually lower than a shop retail price unless the piece is particularly valuable. Items usually have a reserve price put on them by the owner, indicating the lowest price they are willing to accept. If the piece is not sought after, therefore, you may find a piece of furniture that sells at a very reasonable price.

Checking the condition

When looking for wooden furniture, examine every part of the piece, including inside the drawers. Look for woodworm infestation, which can be seen quite easily as small round holes, often in patches. If it is active the holes have a newly bored appearance and traces of wood dust. If you buy any furniture that shows woodworm it can easily be treated by the application of woodworm fluid to eradicate any live worm. It is best to do this outside before taking the piece into the house to prevent any spread of the infestation.

If the wood is dry and cracked and the grain very open, with mouldings split and warped, the furniture may have been out in the rain or kept in a damp place. If it is not already too badly damaged, it can be treated by applying linseed oil and allowing it to soak into the wood.

Dry rot appears in the bottom of furniture pieces; if you touch the wood with your fingers it goes powdery and breaks up. These sections will need to be cut out, the wood treated and the sections replaced with new wood. If there is extensive dry rot leave the piece where it is, however much you like it!

Older furniture is usually made with good solid wooden drawers and wood bases and the furniture itself is usually very sturdy. Most solid wood furniture will strip or rub down, or can be painted. If a small part is broken or missing, check if other parts of the piece, such as the backs of drawers or other parts that will not be seen, have similar wood that can be used for the repair.

Stripping and sanding

You need to know when buying a piece whether it can be stripped or if it is suitable for painting. Any wood painted in a black oil gloss is not usually suitable for stripping but could be rubbed down and painted. Thick primers or oil-based undercoats are often difficult to remove, but most varnished surfaces are easy to strip back and there are several good products on the market especially for this. Many of the new paints can be applied over other paint and varnish layers as long as the piece is prepared correctly. If there are many layers of paint and irregular build-up or peeling, you might find it difficult to obtain a surface good enough to paint on, so the item would have to be either stripped or sanded down well.

You can use a paint stripper, heated gun and a sander to aid stripping. Some pieces can be taken to a professional stripper to immerse in caustic tanks, but this can weaken glue joints and open wood joins. The wood needs to be thoroughly dried out and prepared well by sanding prior to waxing or painting. Paint techniques help disguise blemishes and uneven surfaces; distressed and peeling paint make ideal camouflage.

When refurbishing old wooden furniture you do not need to remove all the underlying colour before applying paint as long as the surface is sanded down to a smooth finish. A good coat of sanding sealer will make sure no old colours or wood stains come through the finished coat.

Paint techniques

All the broken colour techniques, using transparent oil glaze and acrylic glazes can be applied to great effect on almost any piece of furniture, wood and MDF (medium-density fibreboard) as long as the surface has been well prepared and painted with the appropriate base coats, such as primer, eggshells (half undercoat and half gloss) or durable vinyl silk finishes. Oil glaze can be used effectively to transform melamine, Formica and other man-made products, but acrylic and water-based paints cannot.

It is worth visiting your paint supplier and taking some time to find out about the new products being offered. Manufacturers provide plenty of free leaflets giving ideas for product uses, as well as full colour paint charts and useful tips on their use. Many non-toxic, environmentally friendly alternatives are now offered in the form of acrylic and water-based paints and glazing mediums. If you want a sheen finish when using acrylic products you will need a finishing acrylic varnish.

You will need a well-prepared surface with an attractive grain or smooth finish if you intend to use a coloured varnish, furniture wax or thin wood wash, as these are transparent mediums and will show up any defects.

Stencilling has grown in popularity and there are a variety of stencil paints and sticks available, in oil, water-based and acrylic fast-drying paints. Stencils are more effectively applied onto panels and flat surfaces, such as wardrobes, trunks, chests of drawers, tables etc. Even a perfectly plain table can look stunning when painted, stencilled and varnished.

Transforming furniture

Furniture from the middle to the late 19th century is commonly grouped as Victorian. Classic items in this period were painted and elaborately decorated chests of drawers and wardrobes. These were mass produced for smaller houses and cottages, and are today sought after as antiques. During the Victorian era there were also revivals of late Gothic, Renaissance and Rococo furniture, which were richly ornamented and carved mahogany and rosewood pieces. If you have an original piece look after it well and wax it regularly. However, reproductions in less expensive woods are ideal for decorating with paint or for liming.

You can buy quite cheaply a large wardrobe with a flat top, usually found in oak, and transform this easily into a masterpiece in the French armoire style of the late 18th century. Simply fit an ornate top pediment, hand paint designs and create a distressed finish. You can transform a complete bedroom suite in this way by adding flower and bow decorations, gilding and filigree edgings. These techniques can be used on any appropriate furniture, such as bookcases, stools, small tables, screens and whatever else you can envisage.

The same techniques can be used to re-create many other styles of furniture. Scandinavian cupboards also featured pediments although these were not as ornate as the French style. Try re-creating the German dower chests that originated with the settlers in Pennsylvania in the late 18th century, who painted their favourite folk motifs onto natural pine. Similar Austrian and Swiss pieces display designs varying from floral and animal paintings to ornate scrolls. There are many books available with illustrations of designs from all over the world from which you can find inspiration.

I particularly like buying good quality 1950s furniture, as it is well made, often a good shape and inexpensive. You can create your own ageing effect by paint techniques, stencilling and hand-painted designs. Small carved scrolls, wooden decorative pieces and edges that can be added to any plain door or drawers to make a piece more eye-catching and elaborate are available from good wood shops. There are also specialist companies that will cut your designs to order. If you are adept with a jigsaw, try your hand at creating your own pediments, or, if not, commission a local carpenter to do so.

Using your imagination

Before you start searching around junk shops and visiting car boot sales, look around your own home, in your garage, attic and cellar. You may well have a dull-looking wardrobe or other piece of furniture just waiting for a face lift. Junk does not have to be a dirty old bought-in piece – new untreated wood and other small items, new and old, can be transformed just as effectively.

Light fittings can quickly become out of date, so before discarding your old fitting, look at it with a new eye. Can you transform your old brass or metal centre fitting into an elegant verdigris chandelier, or use a pickling technique to revive and enhance a carved wooden one? Your old lamp base can be changed by sponging techniques and take on the look of an antique, the shades changed by decorative finishes. Glass shades could be sprayed with frosted finishes and hand painted. I recently found an old fluted glass lampshade at a car boot sale and hand painted sprays of Victorian-style posies on it as a gift for my mother, copying the flowers from her bedroom curtain material.

Look through your china cupboards. Have you any large jugs that could be given a new life, or decanters and glasses? If you no longer need these they make wonderful gifts once decorated.

Wooden boxes of all sizes are quite easy to find, and a variety of finishes can be created. I have demonstrated a malachite look, but they can be painted, distressed, or covered with découpage to make really useful needlework boxes or to hold jewellery, or wonderful personalized gifts.

terms and techniques

There seems little point in finding an inexpensive bargain, and then spending a great deal of money on the items needed to work on it, so this section outlines only the basic materials used for the projects. Most of us have household tools that can be used, and the few items you do have to buy can be used on many occasions.

Carefully read all the instructions given on containers so that you store them correctly, giving them a long life for use on several projects.

Practise a new paint technique on a painted piece of hardboard or MDF (which can be used repeatedly), until you are happy with the result and feel proficient to use it on your own piece. Oil and acrylic glaze can be wiped off with a damp cloth and white spirit; then you can simply start all over again. If you have left a piece where you have not created enough pattern, or a patch slightly paler than the rest, wait until the glaze is dry to patch it up, or you will end up taking the glaze off and an unsightly ring will appear.

• Acrylic brushes

These brushes are specially made to use with acrylic water-based varnishes. They are made with nylon, and leave the glaze free from brush strokes.

• Acrylic glazing medium (scumble glaze)

This is the alternative to transparent oil glaze, and can be coloured with emulsion or artists' acrylic paint or pigment powder or paint. Full instructions are given on the containers, and it is usually mixed one part paint to four–six parts medium. This glaze has a more matt finish than oil glaze (although you can obtain a sheen using acrylic varnish). There is no odour, it dries quickly and is non-toxic. It can be painted over vinyl silk or acrylic eggshell paint. Ready-mixed cans of glazing medium are available in a large range of colours.

• Acrylic water-based varnish

This varnish is durable, does not yellow with age and is quick drying, so enables you to finish a project quickly. This comes in matt, eggshell and high gloss finishes and you will achieve a better finish if you apply it with an acrylic brush.

• Artists' acrylic paint

This can be purchased in art suppliers and stationers in small and large tubes in a wide variety of colours. Artists' acrylic paints are very versatile and can be used over acrylic or water-based paint. By dipping your brush in water before applying the paint you can float the colour onto the surface, giving a soft delicate finish (often termed as 'floating the colour'). These paints can also be used to colour acrylic glaze, ideal for distressing to create a really old-looking pattern.

I prefer to apply this wax with a clean wad of cloth rather than the recommended wire wool, which can be too harsh for some of the finishes I have created. You can buy different colours, so it is advisable to buy the colour nearest to your finish. Clear wax tends to have a yellowing effect, while neutral is best used with blue and grey shades.

• **Artists' brushes**

Artists' brushes are available in different sizes varying from 00 to 8 or more. A liner has a very pointed tip, and floaters are short or long handled with flat bristles of varying lengths. Many of the projects show photographs of the types I use for different techniques. Artists' brushes are made from hair or synthetic materials.

• **Artists' oil paint**

Artists' oil paints can be mixed with transparent oil glaze and are ideal for hand-painted designs over an oil glaze paint. Dipping your brush in white spirit before applying the paint will act as a thinner. One problem, however, is that these paints take a long time to dry.

• **Black Bison wax**

This is a blend of several waxes and has good resistance to water and finger marks, so is suitable for applying onto painted furniture. It creates a seal for crackled and peeled-paint techniques, and also enhances the ageing effect. Layers of wax and buffing give an attractive sheen.

• **Blu-tack and pink tack (low tack)**

This is widely sold, and can be used to put light articles in place, giving you the advantage of being able to move them around without marking the surface.

• **Broken colour techniques**

This term is used to describe paint techniques with transparent oil and acrylic glazes, such as sponging, stippling, ragging, marbling, colourwashing, graining etc. The techniques I have used are explained in the step-by-step projects.

• Brush cleaners and restorers

There are many kinds of brush cleaner available from hardware and paint stores that quickly remove oil-based paints and varnishes. Use a restorer following the cleaning to soften the bristles and give your brushes a longer life. If you have invested in good quality expensive paintbrushes, it is certainly worthwhile cleaning and restoring them.

• Carbon paper

This paper has a carbon surface on one side, which you place face down onto the furniture. You place the tracing paper, plastic film or photocopied template with the pattern you wish to reproduce, on top of the carbon paper.

• China filler

There is a special china filler called Milliput, which can be purchased at craft suppliers and sometimes at antique centres. Use it to build up small missing areas on edges, and infill cracks and chips. It takes on the appearance of china and gives a fine finish when smoothed off and hardened.

• Crackle and peel medium

A transparent medium applied between two coats of paint to make them react against each other. This technique requires practice and I strongly advise doing so on a piece of hardboard or MDF before you attempt the main large piece. The medium is made by several specialist companies.

• Crackle varnish

This is two varnishes that, when used together, produce a transparent cracked effect. A chemical reaction is triggered when the crackle varnish is applied over the ageing varnish. This is available as both water- and oil-based, so drying times vary.

• Découpage

Découpage means 'cutting'. You can use any pictures, cut-outs, cards and wrapping paper to paste onto an object to create an overall picture. The traditional method was to apply as many coats of varnish as were needed until the edges of the pictures were completely covered and the surface completely smooth. You can buy a special varnish for découpage that is thicker and needs fewer coats, or simply use several coats of clear gloss varnish.

point you must shake well with the cap on before starting your project and during use, as well as maintaining a steady flow by depressing the tip when in use.

• General purpose brushes

Good quality wooden-handled brushes are best and they will give you plenty of service if you clean them well and store them correctly. A good quality brush gives a better finish, but some people prefer to use a cheap brush and throw it away after use. I have bought good quality brushes that are seconds and therefore half the normal price. Continental round brushes are also excellent to use, especially as a substitute for a stippler, and are useful for painting door frames and rounded edges.

• Gesso

This material is made from rabbit skin size and gilders' whiting and used as a preparation before water gilding. It is also used as a preparation for painted furniture when a fine finish is required. Used on unpainted substrates, gesso fills the grain of wood and can be rubbed down to a fine, smooth finish. The recipe for gesso is on page 102 of the malachite box project. Gesso can also be purchased ready to use.

• Gilp

Gilp is made with white spirit, linseed oil and liquid dryers, and is used to seal or prime surfaces for some specialized techniques. The recipe is on page 103 of the malachite box project.

• Dragging brushes

These brushes vary in size and price, depending on the quality of the bristle. They have long hard bristles that are dragged through the glaze to create long, straight, prominent lines.

• Fitch brushes

These very useful brushes have bristles that are flat and angled. You can find one for every purpose, such as for awkward corners or ornate carvings. They are very reasonable in price and the flat wooden handle is also useful for painting straight lines with an artists' liner brush.

• Fixing spray

An artists' spray used for charcoal, pencil and ink drawings to prevent smudging and 'fix' the surface. I also find it useful to stop the bleed in ink photocopies before applying a coat of varnish.

• Flowing ink metallic pens

Metallic pens are obtainable from good stationers and art and craft suppliers. They have diverse uses. As they have a ball

• Gilt cream

This cream is used to touch up gilding on frames and furniture. When the wax is dry you can leave it semi-matt or buff to a shine. It lasts a long time and I use it on many pieces of furniture as a highlighting agent. It is a must in your DIY kit.

• Glass paint

Glass paints are made with resins that not only give them brilliance and transparency, but also durability and adhesion to almost all surfaces. As well as glass, they can be used on most plastics or acetate or stained glass and they are produced in a variety of colours. Test plastic surfaces beforehand to make sure they are compatible with the paint. You can also use spray paints, which are wonderful for creating a frosting effect. You can use glitter glue and gold outlining paint to create interesting designs. Using the outline paint direct from a tube forms an edge, which makes painting the design easy to do and looks extremely effective.

• Glues

Specialist wood and craft glues are available and there are excellent PVA water-resistant glues on the market that dry clear. When using glue, always check on the label that it is suitable for the purpose you intend to use it for.

• Lacquer

Lacquer can be purchased in spray cans or in liquid form to apply with a brush. Always apply several fine coats rather than one heavy coat, which will cause runs and build-up of varnish.

• Lacquer brush

A brush that is specifically for lacquering with thin, flat bristles of ox hair.

• Liming wax

This rich paste wax is formulated to give a white-grained finish. You will need to open the grain of wood first with a wire or bronze brush. Apply the paste with the finest grade of wire wool or a cloth. You can stain the wood with a colour first if you wish and then lime on top. After applying, remove the excess with a cloth and then buff up with a neutral wax to obtain a sheen.

• Low-tack tape

If you need to use tape you must make sure it is low tack to prevent damaging your surface and lifting off paint.

• MDF

Medium-density fibreboard is made from wood thinnings that have been highly compressed to create a smooth finish that is excellent for painting and easy to cut. It is available in different thicknesses and can be bought in various sized sheets; builders' merchants will often cut it to size for you. There are also companies who make special commissions in MDF, including intricate panels and edgings.

• Oil-based paint

Oil-based paint is made up as gloss, eggshell, satinwood, primers, oil glazes, varnishes and artists' oils and is not compatible with water-based paint. You should always read the manufacturer's instructions carefully, as these will give you full details about the paint, its application and drying times. Because of the toxicity of the contents, oil-based paint should only be used in well-ventilated places, handled with care and stored correctly. You will need white spirit for thinning and to clean brushes.

• Oil-based varnish

This is used to protect and waterproof furniture. The more coats that are applied, the more durable the surface becomes.

These varnishes are produced in matt, satin, gloss and high gloss finishes. The high gloss is particularly effective to create a finished lacquer look or on projects such as the malachite box on page 101 and découpage items that require a really high sheen finish. However, this varnish does create a yellowed effect, so if you have a pale-coloured base coat that you wish to retain it is advisable to use a suitable alternative, such as an acrylic varnish.

• Paint kettles, trays and palettes

These are essential for mixing up glazes and colours. You can purchase all of these from decorating suppliers. I save microwavable-food containers, ice-cream cartons (as they have the added bonus of a lid), large and small jars, yoghurt pots and anything else that might come in handy to use. I keep them all in a large cardboard box, so I always have a suitable size container ready for use. I am very keen on recycling and it saves money. You will also need paint sticks to stir your paint, so keep smooth pieces of dowelling, old wooden spoons etc. for this purpose.

• Paint strippers

There are a variety of paint strippers that are readily obtainable. Read the instructions on the container for each one as these will clearly explain its best uses.

• Paintbrushes

After using any brushes, read the instructions on the paint can which explain how to clean them.

• Permanent ink pen

These pens are useful for tracing patterns onto stencil film as they are permanent, do not smudge and create clear outlines. It is essential to use this type of pen as a normal ballpoint pen or pencil will not work on stencil film.

• Pigments

Pigments are derived from natural resources that have been ground to a fine  powder. Earth pigments are natural colours such as ochre, umber, red and sienna and their use dates back to prehistoric times when they were used to create many art forms, including cave and rock paintings. Mineral pigments have also been used as a method of colouring from ancient times, but their sources are now considered semi-precious stones and the colours can be produced synthetically.

Experiment when adding pigment to any medium, as it is very easy to add too much or too little, and create the wrong colour. Take care to mix extremely well to make sure the colour is even and there are no lumps. Make a very small mix first to avoid wasting materials, and when you are happy with the colour, then prepare a larger amount.

• Plastic stencil film

Art and craft suppliers and companies that produce stencils keep plastic stencil film in stock, and it can be purchased by the metre to create your own stencils at a very reasonable cost.

• Primer paint

This is used as the first coat of paint on new wood or surfaces that have been well rubbed down.

• Rabbit skin glue

This is used as a preparation for gesso, a base for gilding, and you can paint it on as a sealer to stop varnish and water penetrating into paper.

• Radiator roller

Radiator rollers are long-handled with very small rollers. They can be purchased from paint and DIY suppliers and you can buy different replaceable roller sleeves depending on what paint you wish to use. Clean the roller sleeves with white spirit (if oil-based products have been used) or warm soapy water (for water-based products). These rollers are ideal for tables, doors and any other flat surface. Their intended use is, of course, to apply paint behind radiators and in confined spaces that are difficult to reach.

• Sanding sealer

You may need to use sanding sealer, which is spirit-based, when you paint new, stripped, dark or heavily knotted wood. It is an excellent sealing base for wood on which you want to apply paper and can be used before waxing on a stripped piece to give a good base for the final wax sheen.

• Sandpapers and glasspapers

You can buy these in strips for a sander, or in sheets in various grades to use for general-purpose sanding. There are different kinds for wood or metal etc. Read the labels to make sure.

• Scalpel

A craft scalpel is ideal for cutting the pattern out of plastic stencil film. It should have a straight-angled blade. They are quite inexpensive and are usually supplied on a card with extra blades. You should change the blade regularly, as you will need a sharp edge when cutting out an intricate pattern. Scalpels are also useful as a craft tool and for scraping away small areas of excess paint.

• Sea sponges

Natural sponges are preferred for sponge techniques as their absorbency and irregular natural structure create attractive patterns. They are quite expensive to buy, so it is worthwhile cleaning them well after use. Look out for sea sponges when abroad, as they are often much cheaper in places where they are found.

• Softener brush

There are many different types of softening brushes, the best being made out of badger hair, although you can buy cheaper alternatives. They are used to soften broken colour work with oil or water-based scumbles, mostly in marbling or graining, and ragging takes on a softer look after using a softening brush to finish.

• Spray mount

This is a widely sold artists' spray adhesive. Use it for lightly putting in place a stencil or drawing, which can be moved repeatedly, until the spray wears off, without causing any damage. Only one thin coat is necessary when recoating.

• Spray paint

Spray paint in easy-to-use cans is readily available in a large range of colours and finishes. Acrylic water-based spray paint specifically intended for use in interior decoration is ideal for almost all surfaces, including wood, metal, plaster, plastic and glass. It can be used for small projects such as stencilling, as the main colour for doors and shutters, and is especially suitable for children's trunks and toys as it is non-toxic. You can also buy spray enamels for metals and glass, pearlized finishes and polyurethane varnishes. Apply the paint in several thin coats rather than one heavy one which will produce paint build-up and runs.

• Stamps for motifs

You can choose from a variety of attractive stamps mounted onto wooden handles. The stamps are easy to use; simply coat with paint using a small roller and apply directly to the surface. Stamp designs are ideal for borders on mirrors and screens. You can order them as a kit from a catalogue or have them created to your own design.

• Stencil brushes

These are specially designed brushes for stencil work. They are round with short, solid bristles to enable you to paint and stipple and there is a wide range of sizes for work with small to large stencils. A double-ended stencil brush is particularly useful when using two colours. There are special stencil brushes for use on fabrics; these have softer and longer bristles, but are not suitable for hard surfaces.

• Stencil paint and sticks

Water-based, acrylic or oil-based stencil paint can be obtained in small pots. Stencil sticks are oil based and wrapped in a sealed film. They can all be blended to make different shades and colours. I find the oils more versatile, as they do not dry as quickly and allow more subtle blending while painting onto the actual stencil itself. Oil paint and sticks can be applied over any surface, whereas the water-based or acrylic paint is more compatible with a water base or acrylic base coat. Stencilling should be a light, soft blending of colours to give highlighted and shaded areas, and

oils enable you to continue working to create this effect, especially over larger areas. Position overlay stencils carefully to avoid smudging the pattern underneath. Do not overload your brush, remembering that paint is easy to apply but sometimes difficult to remove.

• Stippling brushes

Stippling is the term used for finely lifting on or off very fine speckles of paint. Stippling brushes have stiff, dense bristles in a squared-off shape. They are a must for many paint techniques as they have the ability to merge paints and remove hard lines and edges, which is imperative in almost all broken colour techniques. A good quality decorating brush or a round continental brush can be used as a cheaper alternative.

• Tack cloth

A tack cloth is a small, versatile, long-lasting oily cloth that is ideal for cleaning wood, metal, plaster or any other surface (except glass). It will pick up and hold dust and dirt, leaving a completely clean surface to work on.

• Tracing paper

Tracing paper is semi-transparent and can be used for tracing and transferring designs from one sheet to another. You can buy it in sheets or rolls from stationers or craft suppliers.

• Traditional paint

You do not need to apply an undercoat when using traditional paint, which is made with the old pigment colours that were used in 18th and 19th-century matt paint. Traditional paints are water based and several companies now make them in a range of colours to use on their own or mixed together, to create an old-fashioned distemper and limewash finish. They are very versatile and you can paint straight onto wood or any painted surface; you will need to wax or varnish to finish or protect. You can also distress furniture or walls by thinning out the paint with water, which creates a wood wash. I really love using this paint, as it can give any furniture a really aged look.

• Transparent glaze
(Scumble glaze)

Transparent oil glaze is made from linseed oil, dryers, whiting and oils. It is ready to use, which enables you to add your own colour to it, and it is transparent, so to a certain extent the more layers you add the more of a 3-D appearance it takes on. It is used for many paint techniques and broken colour work, for example in marbling, ragging, stippling and many more. It has a long wet, sticky working time that enables you to achieve the desired paint effect and can be used on many surfaces, even man-made ones. You can mix pigments, artists' oils and universal stainers to obtain the colour you require, together with three parts white spirit. You can add a small amount of your eggshell base colour to thicken the consistency. It does, however, yellow with time and ages more rapidly where the surface is not exposed to light. Once the container is opened oil glaze forms a protective skin, but you simply peel this off and stir the glaze.

• Varnish removers

There are a variety of varnish removers that are readily obtainable. Read the instructions on the container for each one as these will clearly explain its best uses.

• Water-based and acrylic paint

Water-based paint is available in many different finishes such as matt, silk, satin and eggshell. These paints are all quick drying, odour free and many are completely non-toxic. Water-based paint is a very adaptable paint for walls, ceilings, furniture and various other uses. A wide range of colours can be changed or

created with water-based artists' acrylic, stainers and pigment colours. Emulsion used on furniture needs a protective finish such as wax or varnish. Water-based spray paints are also available.

• Wet and dry paper

Wet and dry paper is particularly good to use for distressing stencils or hand-painted designs and for smoothing paint surfaces. I use a very fine grade. Do not make it wet, as it leaves black smudges.

• White spirit

This is used as a thinner for oil-based paint and transparent oil glaze, as a cleaner for brushes and to clean or remove spills or splashes of oil-based paint.

• Wire wool

There are various grades of wire wool from very fine (0000) to coarse (00). It can be used for cleaning wood, metal and glass, for applying wax and for cutting back in some distressing paint techniques. Fine wire wool does not scratch or mark wood if used gently and creates a very smooth finish. Soaked in white spirit or warm water it is very useful for cleaning wooden furniture. It is also used with varnish and paint removers, when you should wear protective gloves. Finishing off with wire wool soaked in white spirit removes the small pieces left behind. As wire wool is made out of file steel filaments, cover the floor with paper when rubbing down and throw away the paper afterwards.

• Wood fillers

When filling wood, it is best to buy a specialist wood filler, rather than an all-purpose one. Filler is available in wood colours, as well as plain, and sands down well to a very fine, hard finish. It can be used to fill small holes, cracks, sealing around bad joints and joins in wood.

• Woodworm fluid

Use a proprietary fluid to eradicate any signs of infestation in wood pieces.

glass-fronted
cupboard

This cupboard came from an antique dealer in Ely, Cambridgeshire. It was no use at all to him as it had been painted black and could not be stripped. It was also badly made, with wooden shelves that did not fit properly and was very dirty and covered in cobwebs. The only redeeming feature was the lovely glass-fronted door. The dealer was just about to take the cupboard to a junk shop when I saw it – I bartered with him and managed to buy it for only £10.

I used a 'distressed' paint effect on the cupboard and replaced the wooden shelves with glass ones that were cut to fit. I then carefully cut a hole in the top of the cupboard so that a small, low-wattage spotlight could be fitted. I used decorative wall brackets underneath the cabinet to fix it to the wall.

I first used this stencil several years ago in the corners of a very high Victorian ceiling, and cannot remember where I saw the original design which I based my stencil upon. I have created my own template for you to use (see page 106).

CHECKLIST

- Traditional or emulsion paints in old white, moleskin, yellow ochre and deep rust
- Crackle and peel medium
- Stencil brushes – small and medium
- Stencil or plastic stencil film
- Spray mount
- Gold stencil paint
- Paintbrushes – small and large
- Wet and dry paper
- Pair of wall brackets
- Scalpel
- Permanent pen
- Finishing wax cream

‖ PREPARING THE CUPBOARD AND APPLYING THE BASE COAT

Lightly sand the cupboard, making sure it is clean and free of dust. Using deep rust traditional paint, apply a good coat of dark base all over the cupboard, inside and out, allowing it to dry thoroughly. (This paint does not need an undercoat and can be applied directly onto wood and furniture.) Prepare the brackets in the same way.

- *Applying the dark base coat.*

2 CREATING THE PEELED AND CRACKLED LOOK

Apply a generous coat of crackle and peel medium to the cupboard and brackets and allow it to dry. Do not overbrush, and avoid runs.

• *Applying the crackle and peel medium.*

• *Applying the light top coat.*

3 APPLYING THE TOP COAT

Mix a little yellow ochre with the old white paint to create a pale cream. Apply a generous coat to the inside and outside of the cupboard using bold strokes. Do not overload the brush, and cover the surface as evenly as possible. You will see the 'crackled' look start to take place immediately. Treat the brackets in the same way. Do not go back over the crackled areas or you will lose the effect.

• *Stencilling the design inside the cupboard.*

4 STENCILLING THE DESIGN

Choose or make a stencil (see template on page 106) and apply spray mount to secure it in your desired position. Stencil the design with a gentle, circular motion using moleskin and deep rust paint, taking care to create light and dark areas, then tint small areas lightly in gold. For the aged look, use wet and dry paper, carefully sanding off small parts of the design and sanding down to the base coat in several places to create the distressed effect.

5 FINISHING

Polish with two coats of cream finishing wax.

• *Polishing the cupboard.*

• *A detail of the finished interior of the cupboard, which has taken on a new lease of life as a display case.*

painted
coffee table

Some builders had thrown this delightful oval-shaped coffee table out with the rubbish after renovating a house. It had been partly rubbed down, and the workmen had made it very dirty as they had used it for the duration of their contract. It had elegant, shaped legs with carved grooves and the beading around the top of the table was intact. I was really delighted to find the table in such good condition and asked the builders if I could have it, which caused much mirth as they could not envisage me being able to do anything with it.

I wanted a small coffee table for my living room, and decided on a plain finish with coloured highlighting in a contrast to bring out the shape and patterns. I began by scrubbing the table with warm soapy water to remove all the surface dirt and stains, using a toothbrush to remove the debris from the grooves. I chose a vanilla ice-cream coloured, water-based paint for the main colour and a small packet of Terre Verte pigment powder to mix with this for the detail on the table. When you are painting furniture, it is not necessary to remove all the old colour or varnish, as long as you obtain a clean matt surface to which the new paint can adhere.

Checklist
- Sandpaper – medium and fine
- Clean rag or tack cloth
- 2 paintbrushes – 12 mm (½ in) and 25 mm (1 in)
- Fine longhair art brush (size 1)
- Cream water-based paint
- Terre Verte pigment powder
- Cream furniture wax and a clean lint-free cloth
- Sanding sealer

1 Preparation
Taking care not to damage the surface, rub down the entire table with medium sandpaper, ensuring that any flaking varnishes are removed and the surface is smooth. Repeat the rubbing down with fine sandpaper. Wipe down with a dry cloth. Apply a coat of sanding sealer.

2 Applying the base coats in the main colour
Paint two coats of cream paint, allowing the recommended drying time between coats. You can apply a third coat if needed.

• *Rubbing down the table.*

• *Applying the cream base coat.*

• *Mixing the pigment with the paint.*

• *Painting the top beading.*

• *Highlighting the grooves in the legs.*

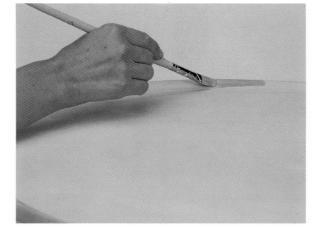

3 MIXING THE PIGMENT

Pour a sufficient amount of cream paint into the lid or a small container and tap out a small amount of Terre Verte pigment powder, mixing thoroughly; at this stage you can add more paint or pigment until you obtain the colour you require. The consistency will be a little thicker than the original water-based paint, but keep it at a workable consistency similar to double cream. Follow the manufacturer's instructions carefully when using the pigment powders.

4 HIGHLIGHTING EDGES AND GROOVES

Using the art brush, apply paint carefully inside the grooves, using long continuous strokes. If the paint does not flow easily, simply dip your brush into water and then into the paint. Using the art brush, paint the top beading with two coats using the same technique and allowing the manufacturer's recommended drying times between coats.

• *Polishing the table.*

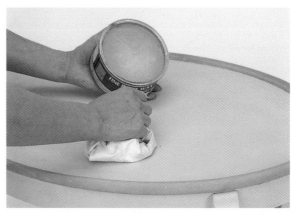

5 APPLYING CREAM WAX AND POLISHING

Using a soft clean cloth, evenly apply the first coat of cream wax to the entire table with a circular motion. Leave for approximately ten minutes and gently buff with a clean cloth. This process should be repeated until you obtain a durable soft sheen finish, but a minimum of two coats is desirable.

heraldic
writing desk

This desk in untreated wood absolutely lent itself to a paint technique. I decided I would hand paint a design on the lid and drawers, and wanted to use one that would enhance the whole appearance of the desk and give it a period look. I finally decided on a mixture of the heraldry, old English hunting dogs and birds that can often be seen on antique tapestries. The dogs have long lean lines and fit in the bottom corners of the lid.

For my colours I chose an oatmeal main base, dragging with an oatmeal glaze, and the designs in washed charcoal, white and ochre. I measured the lid and experimented with small-scale drawings until I was happy with my design. You may have to adjust the template on page 107 to fit the lid size of your own desk. You can photocopy the design, if necessary a part at a time until it is complete. Either trace the design and cut a stencil, or draw a chalk or carbon copy onto the desk itself, and then paint the design in by hand. (If you use a carbon copy you will need to seal with artists' fixing spray before painting to prevent the ink from smudging.) For the drawers I have used the centre piece of the pattern with the crossed long arrows at the same size as the template.

A polyurethane spray varnish over the entire desk creates a good finish and protects the surface and paintings against liquids, scratches and general wear and tear.

Checklist

- Paintbrush – 50 mm (2 in)
- Stipple brush
- Small dragging brush
- Liner art brush
- Small flat artists' brush
- Thin flat piece of wood to draw lines or a long-handled fitch brush
- Small tin of pale primer paint
- Small tubes of artists' oils in charcoal, white, raw umber and yellow ochre
- Oatmeal base coat in oil or acrylic eggshell
- Transparent oil glaze, or water or acrylic-based glazing medium
- Artists' fixing spray
- Carbon or tracing paper
- Soft-leaded pencil
- Paper for template
- Fine glasspaper
- Paint kettle
- Stirring stick
- A small amount of white spirit
- Clean soft cloth
- Spray can of clear polyurethane varnish

❚ Preparation

Wash the writing desk with furniture cleaner and allow to dry. Rub it down with fine sandpaper and wipe off any dust. If you are using a new, untreated wooden piece, then first coat with a primer and allow to dry.

• *Detail of drawer.*

2 APPLYING THE BASE COAT OF PAINT

Remove the drawers and with the 50 mm (2 in) paintbrush cover the entire desk with the oatmeal eggshell base coat and allow to dry for the recommended time. Sand any runs with fine glasspaper. Apply a second coat and allow to dry. Remove the handles and paint the drawers in the same way.

3 MIXING THE GLAZE

Place a spoon of transparent oil glaze into the paint kettle and then squeeze in a tube width of raw umber and half this amount of yellow ochre; stir the paint into the glaze until smooth. Keep adding small amounts of colours in this ratio until an oatmeal colour is achieved. When you are satisfied with the colour (test by dipping in the tip of your finger and rubbing over the eggshell on the side of the desk), add more transparent oil glaze plus white spirit in the ratio of two parts of glaze to one part of white spirit, finally adding one spoon of oatmeal eggshell to the mixture, until you have a sufficient quantity for your project. The stirring consistency should be that of single cream. (I used six spoons of glaze for this project – it is better to make sure that you have enough rather than too little.) The finished mixed glaze should be darker than the base coat.

4 APPLICATION OF THE GLAZE

Begin by painting the back of the desk first, as this will give you the opportunity of using the new glazing technique in a not so obvious place.

Paint the glaze over the back of the desk and stipple immediately with the stippling brush by using a forward and back moderate stabbing motion to remove the brush strokes. Repeat the process over the rest of the desk and drawers. Carry on to the next step immediately.

• *Dragging the oatmeal glaze.*

5 DRAGGING

Starting with the back of the desk, flop the bristle ends of the dragging brush onto the top of the back and gently pull it down in one action to the bottom and off the edge. Continue slightly overlapping in the same manner until you have completed the back. If you have not created the right effect of long straight lines, you can clean off the glaze with a soft damp cloth and white spirit, leaving to dry before reapplying.

Continue in this way for the sides, desk lid and legs, but when you get to the top of the desk and the drawers carry out the process from side to side, rather than top to bottom. Allow to dry for at least 24 hours or until completely dry to the touch.

• *Tracing the design onto the desk lid.*

6 CREATING THE DESIGN

Photocopy the template for the drawers on page 107 and then enlarge it until it is the correct size for your lid (it may be necessary to enlarge onto two separate pieces of paper together to produce the right size). Place a piece of carbon paper, carbon side down, on one side of the lid (a well-used piece will be cleaner to use) and on top of it place the sheet of paper with the design on. Taking care not to put pressure on the carbon paper, gently trace the pattern with the soft lead pencil, using a flat piece of wood or ruler for the straight lines; be careful that the sheet does not move. Peel back the completed side, remove the carbon paper and place it in position on the other side. When you have completed tracing the design on the desk lid, carefully lift off the sheet and then spray the carbon outline with a fixing spray to prevent smudging, and allow to dry.

Using the centre arrow design at its original size from the template, measure the distance between knobs of the drawers and place exactly in the middle. Place carbon paper underneath and using very little pressure trace with the soft lead pencil. Peel off carefully and repeat this procedure on all drawers, using the fixing spray to prevent smudging. Leave to dry.

7 PAINTING THE DESIGN

Squeeze the charcoal, white and yellow ochre paints onto a palette. Pour a small amount of white spirit into the lid of the bottle, and mix very small amounts with the colours to make an easy working consistency. Dip the brush into the yellow paint and paint inside the dogs and the birds. Using the charcoal colour and the liner brush, place the piece of wood or fitch brush along the straight lines and with a well-loaded brush pull

• *Painting the hunting dog design.*

along the edge of the wood and lift cleanly. Continuing with the liner brush and the charcoal, outline the birds, dogs and arrow heads. Blend charcoal and white together and lightly highlight around the edges and small detailed parts. Allow to dry for at least 48 hours.

Paint in the arrow design on the drawers. Allow to dry thoroughly for at least 48 hours. Spray a fine coat of fixing spray over the painted area and allow to dry.

8 VARNISH

Spray with several fine coats of polyurethane eggshell finish varnish, allowing to dry for the recommended time between coats. It is better to apply several fine coats, as one heavy coat will cause runs and build-up of varnish.

Replace knobs and handles as necessary.

• *Detail of desk lid.*

granite effect
fireplace

have never passed a skip without looking inside, as I often find that people are very willing to let you remove any of the contents to give them extra space. I also keep my eyes open when builders are working on properties nearby; wonderful fixtures and fittings are often thrown out.

One day I was passing a house when two builders appeared. They were carrying an old cast-iron fireplace and heading for a skip, so I immediately asked if I could have it. They said that would be fine as long as I could take it away myself. I hailed a taxi and persuaded the driver to take me home with the fireplace, which is now installed in my lounge.

Fireplaces are usually reasonable in cost to have fitted, but make sure you have your chimney checked if you wish to have a real fire.

$\mathcal{C}$HECKLIST

- A cloth
- Sugar soap
- Dark green glitter
- Silver glitter
- Fine black glitter
- Scumble glaze (oil-based or acrylic)
- Sandpaper – medium and fine
- 25 mm (1 in) paintbrush
- Eggshell paint
- Granite paint
- Oil or acrylic tube colours

1 PREPARATION OF THE FIREPLACE

Wash the fireplace with sugar soap solution. Sand the fireplace, first with medium-grade sandpaper, then with fine sandpaper. Using an eggshell paint in a paler colour than your chosen granite paint, apply two coats, sanding with fine sandpaper between each. Be sure to leave the correct drying time between coats.

2 PAINTING THE GRANITE FINISH

Using a 25 mm (1 in) paintbrush, apply the first coat of granite paint (see recipe on page 38). When dry, apply a second coat. I chose a turquoise colour with highlighted pieces in a glittery dark green and silver, which gives a two-tone look that enhances pattern areas.

• *Applying the turquoise paint.*

• *Applying the granite effect paint.*

GRANITE EFFECT PAINT

Place a spoon of transparent oil glaze into a paint kettle and squeeze two tube-widths of monestial green and viridian artists' oil or acrylic paint into the glaze (depending on which scumble you use). Mix until smooth. Keep adding small amounts of colours in this ratio until you achieve the desired colour.

Continue adding more transparent oil glaze plus white spirit in the ratio of two parts glaze to one part of white spirit, finally adding one capful of boiled linseed oil, until you have a sufficient quantity for your project. (Do not add white spirit or linseed oil if you are using acrylic scumble glaze.) The stirring consistency should be that of single cream (I used eight spoons of glaze for this project; it is better to make sure you have enough rather than too little) Stirring all the time, gently tap in the small containers of very fine dark silver and black glitters and one of a medium coarse green glitter. Keep stirring this until it is well worked into the mixture.

Paint on the glaze, and, if you want a more glittery effect, before it is dry put a little fine glitter on a piece of paper and gently blow this onto the surface.

verdigris and crystal chandelier

Verdigris is a term for the natural patina on antique copper in which you can see shades of green with hints of copper tone. Plain brass, metal, plaster and any hard carved or figured surface can be transformed very easily into a beautiful old verdigris effect.

This technique is especially effective with very ornate pieces and I found the perfect one – a brass five-armed ceiling hanging light with raised patterns as well as fine filigree. I was thrilled to find crystal Christmas droplets at the Victoria and Albert Museum shop in London that were ideal for decorating the light fitting, especially as the attachments were brass coloured metal and I could do the same verdigris effect to create an authentic overall look. While on holiday in Alicante, Spain, I visited an antique street market and discovered a box of crystal oddments from an old chandelier. I ordered the glass strands of beads to create the swag effect from a local lighting shop. You can obtain all trimmings for light fittings from good lighting shops or manufacturers.

Light fittings have often been stripped of their electrical fittings for safety reasons, or rewired and labelled accordingly. If the fitting is intact, but not labelled, it is important to have the wiring checked by a qualified electrician.

Checklist

- Bowl of warm soapy water and grade 00 wire wool
- Old toothbrush
- Tack cloth (lint free)
- Clean rags
- Coloured glass paint
- Mid-brown emulsion
- Verdigris kit or pale and dark jade shades of green emulsion
- Gold oil stencil stick or gilt cream
- Round stencil brush (size 2 or larger)
- Small art brush or fitch brush
- Card of fuse wire
- Tape measure
- Small pliers

• *Applying the brown base coat.*

1 CLEANING AND PREPARATION

Fill up a bowl with warm soapy water and, using a small wad of wire wool, thoroughly clean the fitting. Take care to remove all the dirt and dust from between the grooves using the wire wool and an old toothbrush. Wipe down with a wet cloth and then dry with a clean rag. Allow the fitting to dry thoroughly and rub with a tack cloth to remove any remaining particles or dust.

2 PAINTING THE FIRST BROWN BASE COAT

Using the stencil or fitch brush and the mid-brown emulsion, stipple one generous coat over the entire fitting, taking care to cover all surfaces. Allow to dry thoroughly.

3 APPLICATION OF THE LIGHT GREEN EMULSION PAINT

Pour a small amount of light green emulsion into the lid of the can, and firmly dip in the tip of the stencil brush. Work off any excess paint onto a rag or piece of paper kitchen towel. Stipple the paint onto the surface of the fitting over the brown coat, blending carefully so that a fine mottled effect is created. Allow to dry for the recommended time.

• *Applying light green emulsion paint.*

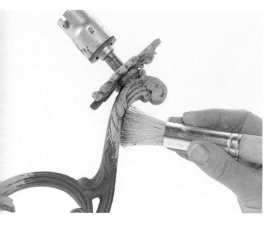

4 APPLICATION OF THE DARK GREEN EMULSION PAINT

With the art brush or the fitch, apply a very small amount of dark green paint to the tip of the brush, wiping off any excess paint. Using light, feathery strokes, highlight the raised patterns and some of the recesses with this dark contrast. This application of paint is to accentuate the line and pattern of the piece to create the aged effect, in contrast to the light green main coat that is left uncovered in parts.

5 HIGHLIGHTING IN GOLD

Using the gold oil stencil stick or gilt wax cream, rub a small amount of gold colour into your thumb and forefinger and then rub into some of the edges, curves, and ends of the fitting.

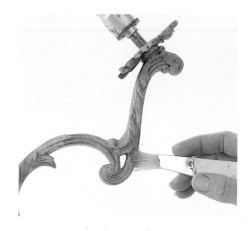

• *Applying dark green emulsion paint.*

• *Highlighting in gold.*

6 ATTACHING DECORATIVE PIECES

Use the same verdigris techniques as described on any decorative pieces you wish to attach, such as leaves, etc. Paint any hanging glass pieces you wish to be coloured with your chosen glass paint and allow to dry before fixing. Measure the distance between the arms of the fitting, allowing at least 5 cm (2 in) extra to create the swag effect of the hanging strands of beads. Attach these to the main droplet loops and then attach to the arms in the required position. Use a small piece of fuse wire if necessary to make a fixing loop (this can be touched up with your art brush later in green emulsion).

• *Attaching the crystal beads and droplets.*

display **decanter** and **glasses**

After finishing the glass illuminated wall cupboard for my living room, I realized I did not have many attractive taller pieces to display, and decided to decorate a decanter and glasses. As I only wanted to display them and did not want to use them for practical purposes, I used spray enamel paint, gold pens and glitter glue, but if you wish to use them as functional objects, you can purchase special glass paints and tubes of colour that are water resistant (see dinner decanter and glasses project on page 45).

Glitter glue is great fun to decorate with. I also chose a pearl and vanilla high gloss spray; this is fast drying and ideal for craft projects, including glass, giving the frosted effect I wanted to achieve. I used the same gold metallic pens as for the calligraphy in the lampshade project on page 98 and the actual piece cut out from the star stencil to draw round for the large design on the decanter and glasses. You can, of course, do this by hand if you wish.

Checklist

- Enamel spray paint
- Glitter glue
- Gold medium-tipped metallic flow pens
- Stencil film
- Permanent pen
- Scalpel
- Newspaper
- Wet and dry paper
- Methylated spirit
- Coloured glass paint (if required)
- Small art brush
- Clean rag cloth

1 Preparation

Wash the glass thoroughly in warm soapy water and dry well. Wipe over with a damp cloth and methylated spirit to remove any excess dirt and allow to dry. Rub over all the surfaces with wet and dry paper and wipe down with a dry cloth.

2 Applying the spray

Cover the surrounding area to protect it. Holding the can of spray paint approximately 30 cm (1 ft) from the decanter and glasses, spray with a thin coat covering all areas. It is best to apply two thin coats rather than one heavy coat, allowing to dry between coats.

• *Applying enamel paint for a frosted effect.*

3 MAKING THE STAR CUT-OUT

Place the plastic stencil film over the large and small stars and the fleur de lys pattern templates, and trace around the outlines with a permanent pen. Cut out with the scalpel and keep the centre of the stars in one piece to use as your pattern outline. The small fleur de lys are just cut out and the centre pieces are not used.

• *Outlining the design with a metallic pen.*

4 GOLD STARS AND FLEUR DE LYS PATTERNS

Very carefully hold the star shape in place with your fingers and draw round this with the gold pen. Read the instructions that come with the pen to make sure that you are using it properly, so that it flows well. (You can use a gold glass paint and art brush if you prefer.) Infill the centre with the gold pen. To outline the fleur de lys, draw round the inside of the design with the gold metallic pen and repeat around the glass base at equally spaced intervals, infilling with silver glitter glue when complete. Allow to dry.

5 GLITTER GLUE AND THE STOPPER

Squeeze the tube of glitter and make a continuous line around the top of the decanter and rims of the glasses, like a sugary cocktail. Swirl around the stopper in a snake design from the bottom to the top, and then with the fine art brush and coloured glass paint create the same pattern following the line of the glitter.

• *Decorating the stopper with glitter glue and glass paint.*

• *Infilling with glitter glue.*

• *Decorated glassware can make good gifts.*

dinner
decanter and
glasses

This decanter and glasses can be used for practical purposes as the special glass paints can be washed without wearing away and are non-toxic. Stunning stained-glass effects can be achieved.

Checklist

- Cloth
- Methylated spirit
- Wet and dry paper
- Gold outliner
- Special glass paint – rose and blue violet
- Squirrel hair art brush

1 Preparation

Wash the glass thoroughly in warm soapy water and dry well. Wipe over with a damp cloth and methylated spirit to remove any excess dirt and allow to dry. Rub over all the surfaces with wet and dry paper and wipe down with a dry cloth.

2 Outlining the design

Squeezing the tube of gold outliner directly onto the glass, make large wiggly shapes. Very carefully hold the star shape in place with your fingers and squeeze an outline around this. Around the top of the glasses use the fleur de lys stencil – and outline these making a line. Leave to dry for ten minutes.

3 Applying the colour

Dip the brush fully into the coloured glass paint and infill the centres of the shapes, alternating the colours.

4 Decorating the stopper

Using the gold outliner, squeeze a swirling line around the stopper from bottom to top, and then with the brush and glass paint create the same pattern as on the decanter.

- *Outlining the design on the glass.*

- *Filling in the shapes with glass paint.*

transforming plain
wooden chairs

I was asked by the owner of a new restaurant to transform some old pine church chairs. She gave me two chairs for samples that had ladder backs, flat tops and the traditional book shelf at the back. She had purchased 80 from a dealer at a very reasonable price, and as they were of very solid wood they would be serviceable for a restaurant.

Old church chairs can be obtained fairly easily from dealers, as they often buy complete job lots from churches, auctions and halls, when they are no longer used. These are usually inexpensive, but once the dealer has stripped and waxed them, the cost increases enormously. Dealers will often negotiate a price for a set, but an odd one also looks very effective and can be decorated to fit in with the décor of any room. I recently visited a dealer's warehouse (a courtesy afforded to you when you become a frequent customer), where there was a huge pile of church chairs for sale, and a set of six was about the price of one new cheap pine chair. If you go to any antique centre, it is worth asking if they have any old church chairs to sell.

I have created four different looks to give you ideas. They are all simple to do and there are templates on pages 107 and 109–10 to help you with your design.

Whenever painting chairs, always turn them upside down first and paint the underside, legs and spindles, and then paint the rest. You should also follow this method on the finishing paint techniques; as well as being easier, it will also give you the opportunity of painting the unseen parts first to give you practice and improve your technique.

Clean the chairs thoroughly before commencing the painting, by sanding first with a medium paper and then a fine one. A coarse or hard sandpaper would permanently scratch and damage the wood. Wash the wood using an old nailbrush or washing-up brush, with a solution of equal parts of warm water and vinegar. You can purchase a furniture cleaner, but this is more expensive. Make sure the wood is thoroughly dry before painting. Also, apply a proprietary woodworm fluid if the chairs show signs of live infestation.

Scandinavian style
scroll chair

Checklist

- Electric sanding machine with/or medium and fine sandpaper
- Soft rags
- Vinegar and water
- Old nailbrush or washing-up brush
- Clear furniture wax
- Art brushes – a fine liner, a short square tip (size 1 or 2), and a floater (size 1)
- Tubes of acrylic artists' colours in Prussian blue, yellow ochre, cadmium yellow, white, black and burnt umber
- Tube of artists' oil paint in raw umber
- Small jar of gilt wax cream
- Flat or round paintbrushes – 25 mm (1 in) and 40 mm (1½ in)
- Traditional furniture paint or emulsion in old white, yellow and deep red
- Tack cloth
- Wood glue
- 2 screws and screwdriver
- Drill
- MDF cut-out scroll
- Fixing spray
- Tracing paper
- Carbon paper

This is the style I created for the restaurant, with a carved scroll attached to the top back of the chair. I found a carpenter to cut the scrolls from MDF (medium-density fibreboard) from a template I provided, but any good timber merchant or carpenter could do this, or you could order them from a company that specializes in cutting designs using your own templates (see Suppliers on page 111). MDF provides an excellent surface for painting.

I decided to paint the chairs with old cream paint and create a crackled, aged look with hand-painted designs and gilt highlights.

For a finishing touch I made padded seat cushions with tassel ties made of jute, natural raffia and gold lurex yarn. When all 80 chairs were in place in the restaurant they looked unusual, stylish and expensive. Several customers commented upon them, asking where they could be purchased as they thought they were original antique hand-painted chairs. The project was a great success.

- *The scroll chair top is cut from MDF.*

1 Creating the scroll chair top

Measure the width at the top of the chair, draw the scroll design to size and make a template on thick brown paper or card. Have the number of scroll backs you need cut out in MDF – you can do this yourself if you are able to use a jigsaw. Drill a hole for a countersunk screw at each end of the scroll and screw it into place to the top back of the chair. It is advisable also to use wood glue on adjoining surfaces.

2 Applying the base coat

Make sure any rough edges are rubbed down with the fine sandpaper after attaching the scroll, then wipe the chair thoroughly with a tack cloth to remove any remaining dust. Paint one coat of old rich dark red traditional furniture paint over the entire chair and leave to dry for the manufacturer's recommended time.

3 APPLYING THE CRACKLE AND PEEL MEDIUM

Paint sections of the chair with the crackle and peel medium but follow the instructions carefully, making sure you do not apply too thick a coat or allow it to run. The parts where you intend to paint your design should be left clear, with small areas surrounding the pattern. Make sure you paint the crackle medium on the flat top and scroll edges to get the desired effect. All the areas that you paint with the medium will crackle and slightly peel when you apply the next coat.

4 TOP COAT

Mix in with old white traditional paint or emulsion, a small amount of yellow ochre (stainer or acrylic) until you obtain an old cream colour, and remember that the final waxing will slightly darken the tone. Using a well-loaded brush, apply the paint in quick even strokes, taking care not to overbrush on crackle areas or you will lose the effect. If there is paint build-up or runs leave until dry as these are dealt with in the next step.

• *Applying the top coat over the crackle and peel medium.*

5 FINE FINISH

With a fine finishing sandpaper or fine wet and dry paper, very gently rub down rough areas and any paint build-up or runs. If there are thin patchy areas, or poor joins between the crackle and main colour, at this stage you can touch up with old cream paint. When dry repeat the sanding process as above. The wet and dry paper will create distressed areas and make visible some of the old red colour underneath, and this is the old distressed effect to aim for.

• *Tracing the design onto the chair back.*

6 TRACING THE DESIGN

Using the template on page 107, copy the design onto tracing paper with a heavy pencil. Place a piece of carbon paper carbon side down on the furniture and, holding the paper pattern on top, trace the patterns lightly onto the painted furniture surface. Spray over with a fine coat of fixing spray.

7 PAINTING THE DESIGN

Using the size 1 flat brush, squeeze a small amount of
yellow ochre, cadmium yellow and white onto a palette
and mix well together to create a pale yellow. Then mix
grey(mix black and white for this), Prussian blue and white
to creat pale blue-grey. Dip the flat brush into water and
side load the paint onto the brush, floating it inside the
patterns. Use yellow for flowers and blue for scrolls.

Using the round brush, shade the flower patterns with
yellow ochre and burnt sienna to outline the edges. Use
the same brush and a slightly darker mixture of grey,
Prussian blue and white to outline one side of the scroll
slopes, then with the fine liner brush paint the finest scroll
lines, outline, swirls and details.

• *Painting the design.*

8 APPLYING THE GOLD GILT CREAM AND BURNT UMBER

Squeeze a small amount of burnt umber into a small container and, using thumb and
forefinger, apply this at random to the edges, joins, corners and scroll tops. Using right
and left thumbs at the top front centre piece of scroll take your thumbs in opposite
directions to make two adjoining semi-circles. This will create the illusion of two carved
separate pieces. Repeat the same process with the gold to create the aged look; you
do not have to apply it too meticulously as smudging enhances the appearance. This
technique looks especially effective when used in parts over the raw umber, giving an
old gold leaf effect.

• *Applying gold to the edges of the chair.*

9 WAX AND BUFF

With a clean rag, apply clear wax evenly
over the entire surface of the chair. Leave
for the desired time before buffing to a
soft sheen.

• *The finished Scandinavian style chair
with painted scroll shape.*

simple folk art style **chair**

It is simple to create a chair that looks as though it has a German or old American origin, by applying bold, colourful paintings in rich earthy colours. The Germans first took their folk art to Pennsylvania in the late 1700s, and traditionally their motifs often depict flowers, leaves and animals intermingled with geometrical designs. Here I show you a basic folk pattern, with a simple ageing technique. To enhance the lines of the chair I attached wooden door knobs to the ends of the flat top.

$\mathcal{C}$HECKLIST

- Electric sanding machine with/or medium and fine sandpaper
- Soft rags
- Vinegar and water
- Old nailbrush or washing-up brush
- Clear furniture wax
- Art brushes – a fine liner (size 1) and a flat (size 1)
- Tubes of acrylic artists' colours in red, Prussian blue and yellow ochre
- Flat or round paintbrushes – 25 mm (1 in) and 40 mm (1½ in)
- Traditional furniture paint or emulsion in old white and deep red
- Crackle and peel medium
- Card
- Scissors
- Tape measure
- Pencil
- Tack cloth
- 2 wooden door knobs
- 2 double-ended screws
- Wood glue

1 PREPARATION

After rubbing down the chair with fine sandpaper, fix a small wooden door knob at each end of the flat chair top in line with the sides of the back of the chair, using a double-ended screw and wood glue. You need to drill a hole in the appropriate position in the top of the chair and screw the double-ended screw into the hole with pliers. You can then screw the knob into place. You may be able to purchase wooden knobs with a screw already in place, and then you can screw directly into the drilled hole. Wipe away any excess of wood glue with a dry cloth. Sand any rough edges with fine sandpaper and dust down with a tack cloth.

2 APPLYING THE BASE COAT

Paint one coat of old rich dark red traditional furniture paint over the entire chair and leave to dry for the recommended time.

- *Screwing the knobs into the top of the chair.*

3 APPLYING THE CRACKLING MEDIUM

Paint sections of the chair with the crackle and peel medium following the manufacturer's instructions carefully. Make sure you do not apply too thick a coat or allow any runs. The parts where you intend to paint your design should be left clear with small areas surrounding the pattern. Make sure you paint the crackle and peel medium around the flat top and on parts of the door knobs to obtain the desired effect. All the areas that you paint with the medium will crackle and slightly peel when you apply the next coat.

4 TOP COAT

Mix in with old white traditional paint or emulsion a small amount of yellow ochre stainer or artists' acrylic until you obtain an old cream colour. Remember that the final waxing will slightly darken the tone. Using a small well-loaded brush, apply the paint in quick even strokes, taking care not to overbrush on crackle areas or you will lose the effect. If there is paint build-up or runs, leave until dry as these are dealt with in the next step.

5 FINE FINISH

With a fine wet and dry paper very gently rub down rough areas and any paint build-up or runs. If there are thin patchy areas, or poor joins between the crackle and the main colour, at this stage you can touch up with the old cream paint. When dry, repeat the sanding process as above. The wet and dry paper will create distressed areas and make visible some of the old red paint colour underneath and this is the old distressed effect you are aiming for in the decoration.

6 HAND PAINTING THE FOLK ART
PATTERN

Cut a semi-circular piece of card to fit the inside middle of the flat top of the chair, between the knobs, leaving a clearance distance around the semi-circle of approximately 2.5 cm (1 in). Hold this in place and with the fine artists' liner brush paint a line of blue around the semi-circle side of the template, and the flat edge vertically down the back slats as shown. Squeeze small

• *Using a semi-circular piece of card as a guideline for painting.*

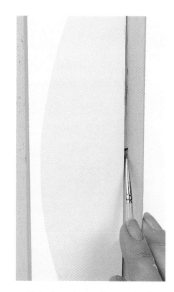

• *Painting down the vertical edges of the slats.*

• *Painting the outlines of the leaves.*

amounts of each colour onto a palette. Paint the outline of three pairs of coloured leaf-shaped patterns, alternating the colours between the Prussian blue and yellow ochre (as shown). Paint the outline of a small bud-shaped design at each end of the pattern in tomato red with Prussian blue leaves.

7 FLOATING IN THE COLOUR

Using a small amount of water with the paints, mix a little white paint with your main colours to create a paler tone and fill in the pattern. Then side load the brush without water with the darker shade, using one bold stroke around one side of the outside edge over the paler colour, to make a contrast shaded effect. Leave to dry for the manufacturer's recommended time. Repeat as desired on the other back slats of the chair, adapting your template accordingly.

• *Mixing your colours on the palette.*

8 CREATING THE AGEING EFFECT

Squeeze a small amount of Prussian blue into a small lid or container and, using thumb and forefinger, apply this at random to the corners, edges, wood joins and knobs. Allow to dry and then repeat the same process with the gold gilt cream.

• *Distressing the paint with sandpaper.*

9 DISTRESSING THE PAINTED PATTERN

Check that the paint is completely dry before distressing. Using a fine wet and dry paper in very gentle up and down movements, sand off small areas of the pattern to create the aged distressed look.

10 WAX OR VARNISH TO FINISH

With a clean rag, apply clear wax evenly over the entire surface of the chair and leave for the desired time before buffing to a soft sheen. Alternatively, using a small varnish brush, apply two coats of varnish, allowing drying time between coats.

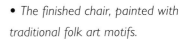

• *The finished chair, painted with traditional folk art motifs.*

Oriental lacquered **chair**

The inspiration for this chair came to me when my daughter returned home from an outing with her Grandma to see the pantomime *Aladdin*. She was wearing a coolie hat decorated with a dragon and oriental calligraphy. I photocopied the designs, cut them out and used them for a simple découpage. Any suitable patterns of your choice could be used in this way or you could create your own hand-painted designs; I chose the simple alternative.

You can buy coloured or clear lacquer that is specially made to create the Eastern lacquerware finish; alternatively, you can use high gloss varnish or acrylic glaze to obtain the same effect. The use of bright festive red, along with black and gold, is popular in traditional oriental lacquering. These lacquers were originally made from tree sap, but they are now produced using synthetic materials.

*C*HECKLIST

- Fixing spray
- Sufficient photocopies of oriental paper patterns
- Bright red eggshell paint or gloss
- Tube of black artists' oil paint
- Small sharp-pointed scissors
- Craft glue
- Lacquer
- Varnish brush
- Small paintbrush

1 PREPARING THE PAPER PATTERN

Photocopy the number of patterns you will need and some spares, making sure you reverse some of the dragons (see template on page 109); you will need three pairs of dragons. Also photocopy an assortment of characters and small pieces for the narrow sides of the chair. Cut out all the designs carefully, using a small pair of sharp-pointed scissors.

2 APPLYING THE BRIGHT RED PAINT

Turn the chair upside down and paint the underside and legs of the chair first. Then stand it the right way and paint the complete chair. Allow for the manufacturer's recommended drying time and then apply a second coat of paint.

3 GLUING CUT-OUT PATTERNS

Decide where you wish to place the designs and characters, apply the craft glue to the back of the cut-outs and stick them in place. I placed a pair of dragons on the top of the chair, a pair on the front of the rail and a pair on the back. Dab over with a clean cloth to remove any surplus glue and press firmly to adhere to the chair. When dry, spray one good coat of fixing spray over each design to prevent any bleeding of ink.

• *Painting the chair with bright red paint.*

• *Gluing the designs to the chair.*

• *Burnishing the chair with black oil paint.*

4 BURNISHING THE CHAIR

Remove the cap from the black artists' oil paint, and pass your thumb over the top of the tube to obtain a very small amount and rub onto your thumb and forefinger. Smudge this along the edges and into the joins of the chair to create an aged, burnished appearance. It looks very authentic if you also apply this smudging to the edges and parts of the seat that would have been well worn and sat in. Some chairs have an indentation in the seat that you can highlight in this way.

• *The lacquer finish enhances the depth and gloss of the red paint.*

5 LACQUER FINISH

With a small varnish brush, apply two coats of lacquer or high gloss alternative, allowing the manufacturer's recommended drying time between coats. Allow the lacquer to harden before using the chair.

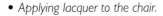

• *Applying lacquer to the chair.*

Shaker style **chair**

Shaker-style furniture originates from the early American settlers and has become extremely popular. Its simplicity is appealing and the furniture is now produced commercially by large companies, in pale, natural and muted colours such as linen, jute and duck-egg blue. Originally the chairs were hung up on the walls when not in use. Simple flower and heart motifs were cut out of the woodwork, creating a basic, uncluttered décor that blended in with a plain and simple environment.

If you are worried about transforming chairs, and deciding what will fit in with your existing decorations, you will find that the minimalist look of Shaker style blends in well with most rooms, and it is easy to adapt the colours you wish.

This church chair is made over in duck-egg blue with a very simple hand-painted flower motif that anyone can tackle. When choosing your main colour of paint, bear in mind that the final waxing will tone down the colour to a slightly darker shade (a good way to test this is by licking your finger and pressing it onto the painted surface before waxing, and this will show the approximate finished colour). You will need neutral wax on the blue paint as it has a slightly grey tone that complements blue-grey shades.

1 PREPARATION

Clean the chair thoroughly with a good furniture cleaner, or a solution of equal quantities of vinegar and water, then leave to dry. Sand down using medium and then fine sandpaper, and if necessary treat for woodworm with a proprietary fluid.

2 MIXING YOUR OWN COLOUR

Pour half the old white paint into the paint kettle and add a very small amount of the dark blue traditional paint, stirring thoroughly and gradually add more until you obtain the pale blue you require. It is very difficult if you have put too much of a darker colour in to make it lighter again, so it is advisable to take your time when mixing the paint.

CHECKLIST

- To mix your own duck egg blue you will need traditional or pigment paint in old white and dark blue, a paint kettle and a mixing stick
- **OR** use a ready-mixed pale blue water-based paint
- 50 mm (2 in) paintbrush
- Fine liner art brush (size 0)
- Fine art brush
- Artists' acrylic paints in Prussian blue and white
- Tub of neutral furniture wax
- Clean soft cloth
- Medium and fine sandpaper

• *Applying the first coat of paint to the chair.*

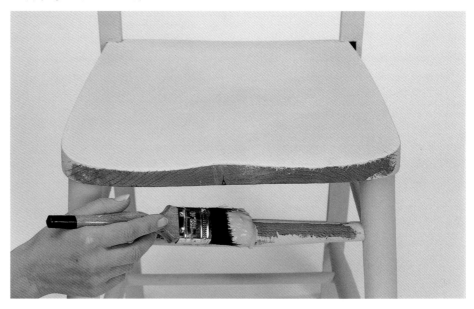

3 APPLYING THE MAIN COLOUR

Apply two coats of the blue paint over all the surfaces of the chair, turning the chair upside down and painting the underside and legs first. Allow the manufacturer's recommended drying time between coats.

4 HAND-PAINTED FLOWER MOTIF

Squeeze two small separate amounts of Prussian blue and white artists' acrylics onto a palette. Dip your liner brush into water and put a little bit of blue and white together on a separate part of the palette and mix together until you make a third colour of pale blue. Decide where you wish to paint your motif on the chair and, using the pale blue paint, create a small circle for the middle of the flower and five petal shapes for the leaves around the centre.

Dip a fine art brush into the Prussian blue and outline one edge of each leaf and the centre. Leave to dry for the manufacturer's recommended time.

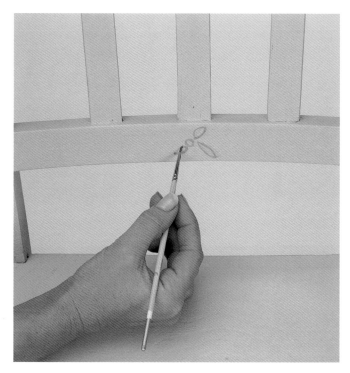

• *Painting the petal shapes of the flowers.*

5 WAX FINISH

Make a wad with a soft clean cloth and rub it well into the neutral furniture wax. Using a circular movement, gently apply the wax to all surfaces of the chair and buff. Apply at least two coats until you have an even, soft sheen.

• *Applying the wax with a soft cloth.*

• *The simple decoration on this chair can easily be adapted for other pieces.*

• *Buffing the waxed surface for an even sheen.*

vine leaf
table

My mother asked me if I could transform her round dining table and lighten its colour so that it did not dominate the room. She wanted it to be practical, but to enhance the room when not in use.

I wanted to create a table that would look good in the daytime and even better for an evening dinner. It is a good functional table, with round edges, and can also be extended with a middle leaf. You need to take this into account when measuring for a centre pattern. You can use a varnish remover to strip the table and full directions for using this are given on the container. Many modern paints can be applied to various old finishes, but it is always better to rub down surfaces beforehand to obtain a good key so that the paint adheres. You can apply several coats of acrylic glaze or varnishes to preserve your painted design on the table and obtain a durable finish.

I first painted the table in a rich cream eggshell base coat, and prepared a butterscotch glaze to create effective swirling patterns. I decided to decorate the table by stencilling large bunches of grapes with leaves as a centrepiece, and a twining vine leaf pattern around the edge.

Checklist

- Transparent oil glaze
- White spirit
- Large spoon
- Artists' oil paints in burnt umber and yellow ochre
- Cream eggshell paint
- Stipple brush
- Clingfilm
- Acrylic glaze, satin or gloss
- Radiator roller with sleeve for oil-based paint
- Plastic stencil film
- Spray mount

- Stencil oil sticks in wine red, deep blue, leaf green and dark emerald green
- Permanent fine-tip pen
- Scalpel and blade
- Paint kettle
- Sander or wood sandpaper in medium and fine grades
- Fine wire wool
- Varnish remover
- Paintbrush 50 mm (2 in)
- Tack cloth
- Fine glasspaper or finishing paper
- Tape measure

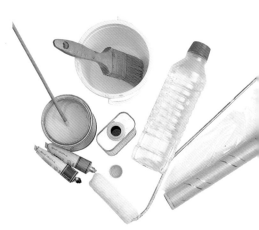

1 PREPARATION

Remove old varnish and dirt with a good varnish remover, and sand down first with medium and then with fine sandpaper. Rub down gently with fine wire wool soaked in white spirit to remove all debris and leave to dry. Wipe down with a tack cloth.

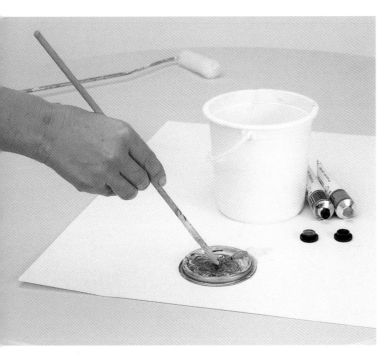

• *Stirring the oil paint into the oil glaze.*

• *Applying the butterscotch glaze.*

2 APPLYING THE MAIN COAT

Turn the table upside down and paint the underside and legs in cream eggshell. Allow to dry before applying a second coat and when dry turn the table the right way up. If you complete the underside and legs first, it means you can then concentrate on working on the top surface. I used a radiator roller with a sleeve for oil-based paint for the large flat top, as this eliminates any chance of brush strokes, as well as being quick to do and creating a really good smooth surface for paint techniques. When the first coat is dry, very gently and lightly sand the top with finest glasspaper to remove hairs and any paint particles. Apply a second coat in the same way. If a good cover has not been obtained with two coats, you may need to apply a third, sanding in between each coat. Allow to dry for the manufacturer's recommended time.

3 MIXING THE BUTTERSCOTCH GLAZE

Place a spoon of transparent oil glaze into the paint kettle and squeeze into it a tube width of yellow ochre and half this amount of burnt umber oil paint. Stir this into the glaze until smooth. Keep adding small amounts of colours in this ratio until a butterscotch colour is achieved. When you are satisfied with the colour (test by dipping in the tip of your finger and rubbing over the eggshell on the underside of the table), continue adding more transparent oil glaze plus white spirit in the ratio of two parts glaze to one part of white spirit, finally adding one spoon of cream eggshell to the mixture until you have a sufficient quantity for your project. The stirring consistency should be that of single cream. (I used eight spoons of glaze for this project – it is better to make sure that you have enough rather than too little.)

4 APPLICATION OF
THE GLAZE

Paint the legs of the table first as
this will give you the opportunity
of using the new technique in a
not so obvious place.

Paint the butterscotch glaze
over the legs of the table, and
stipple immediately with the
stippling brush by using an up and
down moderate stabbing motion to
remove the brush strokes. Repeat the
process over the top of the table.
Continue on to the next step immediately
you have done this.

• *Stippling over the butterscotch
glaze.*

• *Drawing around the outline of the
template.*

5 CREATING THE SWIRLING EFFECT WITH CLINGFILM

Cut pieces of clingfilm approximately 30 cm (12 in) square. Taking each square between
the thumb and forefingers of each hand and holding it 30 cm (12 in) above the surface,
lean over the table and blow into the centre of the clingfilm, allowing it to float down
onto the table. Blow over all the areas of the clingfilm while it is stuck onto the glaze.
Gently peel one corner and pull off in one movement. Repeat this evenly all over the
table, overlapping slightly so that parts are not missed and no hard edges are left. Repeat
the process on the legs of the table. Change the film frequently when it becomes loaded
with glaze. Leave overnight to dry.

6 MAKING THE STENCIL

Place stencil film over the template on
page 108 and draw around the outlines
with the permanent pen (this will not rub
off). Cut these lines with a scalpel. There
are five pattern pieces: leaves with two
grapes, two separate grapes – one large
and one small (cut these two on a
separate 15 cm/6 in square piece of stencil
film), and two vine twists.

7 POSITIONING THE DESIGN

Measure a circle in the centre of the table
and position your stencil, equally spacing
the large bunches of grapes (using the
pattern piece of leaves with two grapes as
the starting point), and then building up
smaller bunches in between (using the
two separate grapes).

• *Using clingfilm to create a swirling effect
on the table.*

8 STENCILLING THE CENTRE DESIGN

Spray a light coating of the spray mount onto the back of the stencil and place it in position. Cut a small square section of plastic and rub all of the stencil oil sticks in their own corners to break the transparent seal covering the stick. This leaves paint on the plastic, which becomes your palette. Work the stencil brush into the leaf green colour and stipple this with a circular motion into the leaf part of the design. Work into the brush a small amount of the dark green and stipple around some edges for contrast shading. With a separate brush, use just the wine red for the main two bunches of grapes. Proceed only using this pattern piece until the circle is complete.

• *The grapes are stencilled overlapping each other to make a bunch.*

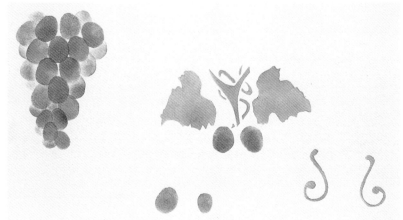

• *Practise building up your design on paper first.*

9 CREATING BUNCHES OF GRAPES

I bought a bunch of grapes and practised building up a bunch on a piece of paper before I actually started the stencil on the furniture. I have stencilled a bunch of grapes for you as a guideline (see above). You will see that I have stencilled odd half grapes to give the bunch a good shape at the edges and so that the bunch tapers to the end.

The red and blue mixed together make purple to shade the darker grapes and edges. Starting at the top of the bunch, with the two top grapes as a guide, stencil the large grape on the outside and slightly below to create a cluster effect. Keep the colour light and transparent at this stage, so you can layer over existing grapes, which will give you a 3-D effect. After you have stencilled approximately five large grapes downwards, change to the smaller grape and stencil four or five irregularly to create the tail of the bunch. Mix the darker purple and shade the top surface grapes to bring them into the foreground. Oil paint takes some time to dry and harden completely, so leave sufficient time for this to take place, approximately 48 hours or longer if required.

Depending on the shape of your table, you may wish to add further bunches of grapes as part of your centre design – I have stencilled a miniature bunch between the large ones using the small grape pattern only.

• *Overhead view of the table top showing grape and foliage patterns.*

• *Varnishing the table with acrylic glaze.*

• *Stencilling the vine leaf border.*

10 CREATING THE BORDER ROUND THE OUTSIDE OF THE TABLE

Using the main stencil pattern, stick a small piece of plastic with the spray mount over the grapes and the vine stalk in the centre of the leaves as you will be using only the leaves for the border. Stencil one leaf next to the outside edge creating an outward leaf with an inward twine followed by an inward leaf with an outward twine (see photograph above).

11 ACRYLIC GLAZE VARNISH

If you use an oil-based varnish it will create a yellowed appearance and spoil the colours in your design, so it is preferable to use several layers of acrylic clear-glaze varnish. Glaze can be bought in matt, satin and gloss finish depending on your preference.

Using an acrylic glazing brush, paint over the legs and table surfaces several layers of acrylic clear-glaze varnish, allowing the manufacturer's recommended time between coats. This will go on as a milky consistency, but will dry to a transparent finish. Do not overbrush as the glaze dries very quickly.

pine panelled
cupboard

𝒞HECKLIST

- Scalpel
- Ruler or tape measure
- Small jar of black patina or charcoal
  oil paint
- Clear wax
- Clean lint-free cloths
- Print or paper designs
- Crackle varnish
- Wallpaper paste or home-made paste
  from flour and water
- Blu-tack
- Rabbit skin glue
- Small container
- Small varnish brush
- Bowl of vinegar and water
- Sanding sealer
- Scissors

bought this cupboard some time ago and it had already been stripped and was in good condition, but with no waxing or finish. Our television had been sitting on it since we moved while I waited for inspiration on how to make the cupboard more attractive, without spoiling the natural old pine. Original old pine furniture is sought after, and quite expensive, so I felt it would be a shame to change the look of the natural wood.

I was coming home one day after working on the refurbishment of the Royal Albert Hall, and passed several shops with prints of old pictures, pages from books and wrapping paper and this gave me the idea of putting something similar into the panels of the doors. I then thought how wonderful the pictures would look if I aged them with a crackle varnish to make them look really authentic, like Old Master paintings.

I searched through the posters and prints looking for something appropriate for a kitchen and that would blend in with the antique pine wood. I found these old 18th-century French prints underneath a pile in a drawer and thought they would be absolutely perfect. 'Le jardinier' (the Gardener) was made up of fruit, vegetables and garden implements, and 'La confiseuse' (the Confectioner) was similarly designed with sweets and cakes. They are part of a set called 'Tradesmen in Costume', and I later discovered that the dancer Rudolf Nureyev had also displayed the whole set in his Paris apartment.

To wax pine furniture use a cream or pine-tone wax, applying several coats if necessary, buffing well until you achieve a soft sheen. I bought four wooden door knobs and attached these to the bottom of the cupboard to make it floor standing and polished these in the same way. Beeswax is excellent for reviving old wood, nourishing it as well as protecting the surface.

1 CLEANING AND PREPARATION

Mix equal parts of warm water and vinegar in a bowl, then wash the cupboard with the solution, using a nailbrush or soft scourer to remove any stains and surface dirt. Wipe off with a soft cloth and clean water and leave to dry.

2 SEALING THE PANELS

Paint a coat of sanding sealer on the surfaces to which the pictures will be pasted. This prevents any seepage from the wood penetrating the paper and creates a good surface for the glue. Leave to dry for the manufacturer's recommended time.

3 FITTING THE PICTURES INTO PLACE

Cut the paper to the size of the panels. Place it in position with Blu-tack until you are sure it is in the right place. Carefully trim off any excess edges.

4 PASTING THE PICTURES INTO POSITION

Follow the manufacturer's instructions on how to mix the paste, and apply it evenly to the back of the picture. Paste the picture into position using a dry paste brush or soft cloth, smoothing from the middle to the outer edges to release any air bubbles. Wipe off any excess paste. Allow to dry thoroughly.

• *Applying sanding sealer to the panels.*

• *Applying rabbit skin glue.*

• *Measuring the pictures prior to cutting to size.*

5 MAKING AND APPLYING THE RABBIT SKIN GLUE

If you are using a black and white picture that has been photocopied or is not good quality it is wise to spray with an artists' fixing spray to stop any possibility of bleed.

Mix 16 parts rabbit skin glue to 1 part moderately hot water and keep stirring until all the pieces are dissolved. While still warm, paint a generous coat over the picture with a well-loaded brush and leave to dry. This forms a protective coating over the print and stops the varnish penetrating into the paper.

6 APPLYING THE AGEING AND CRACKLING VARNISH

Try the following technique on another picture that does not matter before attempting the real one. You will then know how long to leave the crackle varnish as this varies with the temperature of the room; it will also give you the opportunity of practising how to obtain the desired ageing effect.

Paint on a coat of the ageing varnish and leave until still wet, but not sticky to the touch. In order to obtain the large cracked appearance you need to wait 1 to 1½ hours and to obtain the small cracked appearance you need to wait to a maximum of 3 hours before applying the crackling varnish. Drying times vary with the temperature and humidity of the room. If the surface does not crackle after one hour, use a warm hairdryer to blow gently onto the surface of the varnish, but do not carry on once it begins to crackle. Allow to dry thoroughly. There are oil and acrylic water-based crackles, so read the instructions supplied for the correct timing.

7 TO INTENSIFY THE CRACKLED LOOK

Apply a small amount of black patina or thinned charcoal artists' oil paint onto a clean cloth and rub over the dry varnish, then wipe off straightaway. As an alternative you can also apply gilt cream to the surface.

You can finish off with a final coat of ageing varnish to obtain an attractive sheen if preferred.

• *Applying the crackle varnish.*

• *A detail of the finished crackled effect on the panels of the cupboard.*

shutters and louvre doors

I chose a non-toxic acrylic spray paint for these shutters and louvre doors, as slatted strip doors and other intricate wood finishes are time consuming and laborious to brush paint; it is often difficult to get into the numerous corners and avoid runs and paint build-up. A wide range of colours is available in spray paints; some companies make safe non-toxic sprays specifically for children's furniture and toys. I chose turquoise blue and a burnt sienna (rust colour) for the spattering or fine speckled look. Spray and spattering is great fun, but best done out of doors, or in a well-ventilated space, making sure all surrounding areas are thoroughly covered to protect them. It is all too easy to create a speckled image over yourself as well, so it is a good idea to cover yourself up well.

I mounted the shutters with door hinges, and completed the look with brass sea-horse handles.

• *Sanding down the old paint surface.*

CHECKLIST

- 3 cans of turquoise blue acrylic spray paint
- Spray polyurethane varnish in satin finish
- Small pot of burnt sienna water-based paint or tube of artists' acrylic
- Large long-bristled art brush
- Stick or old brush
- Paintbrush – 40 mm (1½ in) or 50 mm (2 in)
- Electric sander with/or sandpaper in medium and fine grades

I PREPARATION

Wash the doors thoroughly with warm soapy water or sugar soap. Leave to dry. Thoroughly sand down all surfaces to remove flaking and peeling pieces of old paint or varnish. Wipe over.

2 SPRAYING COLOUR

Shake the can of decorative paint before use. Hold it approximately 30 cm (1 ft) away from the door and spray evenly over one side of the entire door. A better finish is obtained by repeating several thin coats rather than trying to cover with one heavy coat, which will cause runs. When dry, turn the shutters

upside down and repeat. Turn horizontally and spray all uncoated edges, then turn again and repeat. Repeat this process on the other side of the door. When you have achieved an even cover leave to dry for the manufacturer's recommended time.

• *Spraying the turquoise blue paint onto the door.*

3 SPATTERING IN BURNT SIENNA

The burnt sienna paint should be watered down slightly to achieve the spattered effect. Practise dipping the tip of the art brush into the burnt sienna paint, and knocking it against a stick or another long-handled brush, as shown in the photograph, onto an old card or paper until you can judge how much paint you need to spatter small specks onto the surface. Be careful not to overload the brush. When you have mastered the technique apply spattering to all sides of the doors. Allow to dry for the manufacturer's recommended time.

• *The sea horse handles.*

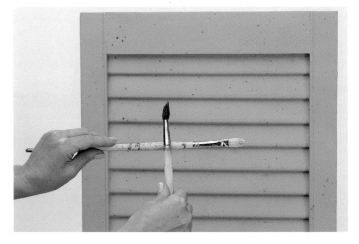

• *Spattering the burnt sienna paint onto the painted door.*

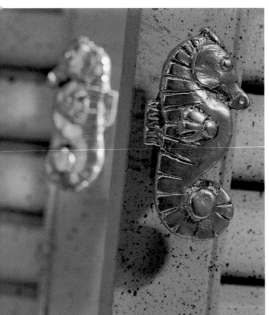

4 SPRAY VARNISH

Spray a fine coat of polyurethane varnish over the entire surface of the doors and shutters. Allow to dry for the manufacturer's recommended time, then repeat with another coat of varnish.

• *Varnishing the door using a spray.*

bathroom **cupboard**

After much searching I found this small glass cupboard in old pine with a tarnished mirror at the back, which adds to the character of the piece. The wood had already been stripped, but the finish was poor, and there were damaged parts to fill. I decided a thin woodwash would enhance the overall appearance and let the grain of the wood still show through. I distressed the cupboard with wet and dry paper to bring out the grain, concentrating more on some edges than others to cut back to the natural pine.

As I used seahorse handles on the louvre doors and shutters (see page 70), I made a sea horse and skeleton fish stencil to spray onto the glass door and sides of the cupboard, so that the mirror on the back would reflect these effectively. Then I used the stencil to create a decorative border around the wall and to frame the shutters in the window. The templates are on page 108.

I had a piece of glass cut for a shelf and used two wrought-iron hanging basket brackets sprayed with gold paint. You can transform any shelf brackets in this way. The glass shelf should be glued onto the brackets.

For the lower part of the bathroom walls I made up a raw sienna coloured paint. I used a 50 mm (2 in) paintbrush with an up and down stroke, then pulled the brush up the entire surface to create a soft grain look (see page 69).

❧ CHECKLIST

- Pale jade emulsion paint
- Plastic stencil film
- Permanent pen
- Can of spray paint
- Paper masking tape
- Scalpel
- Spray mount adhesive
- Tape measure
- Clean rags
- Methylated spirit
- Small amount of white spirit
- Wet and dry paper or fine wire wool

I PAINTING THE BASE COAT

Water down the pale jade emulsion with equal parts of water to paint. Paint this onto all the wooden surfaces of the cupboard as a woodwash (you can see the grain of the wood clearly through the wash). Allow to dry thoroughly.

- *Applying the base coat of pale jade emulsion.*

• *Cutting back the paint with wet and dry sandpaper.*

2 CUTTING BACK

With wet and dry sandpaper or fine-grade wire wool, gently rub over the painted surfaces so that there are areas of the pine and the grain showing through in their natural state, and the surface is smooth. When thoroughly dry, apply a coat of neutral furniture wax or liming wax and buff to a soft sheen.

3 PREPARING THE GLASS

Put a small amount of methylated spirit onto a clean lint-free rag, then thoroughly clean the mirror and glass of the cupboard. Polish off and allow to dry.

4 MAKING THE STENCILS

Using the templates on page 108, place the plastic stencil film over each pattern separately and trace the outlines with a permanent pen. Cut out the seahorse and fish with a scalpel on individual pieces of stencil film.

5 POSITIONING THE STENCIL

Carefully plan and measure the distances between alternating patterns of the seahorse and the fish, with equal spacing. I placed fish at the top and bottom and the seahorses up the sides of the glass front of the cupboard, to show complete stencils between shelves. If this is your first attempt, try the stencil on paper first.

6 SPRAYING THE STENCIL

Spray the front of the stencil with mount adhesive (as this will be placed onto the wrong side of the glass in the reverse position). Stick it in place and mask off the rest of the glass with paper and masking tape. Holding the spray 30 cm (1 ft) away, spray as a fine mist in one sweeping left-to-right motion; heavy application will leave runs of paint and the stencil will not peel off cleanly. Wipe excess paint off the stencil using a clean cloth and white spirit. You can scrape off any smudged paint quite easily with a scalpel when dry.

• *Cutting out the stencil with a scalpel.*

• *Planning the effect of the stencils on card.*

• *Spray painting the stencil.*

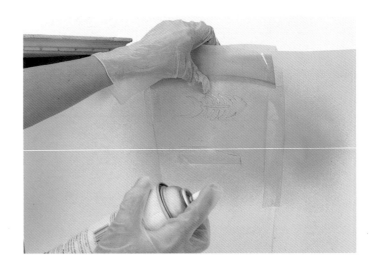

wardrobe and headboard

began looking for a wardrobe with an ornate scrolled top and panels to decorate, but all those I found were expensive. Second-hand flat-top wardrobes are obtainable at a reasonable cost, however, and I realized that if I designed my own pediment, I could then attach it to the wardrobe. I soon found a suitable large, Victorian, mahogany wardrobe in a local junk shop.

Once I had measured the top and sides of the wardrobe and produced a drawing of the pediment I wanted (see page 109), I sent it to a company who would make it up to my design. They quickly returned a proof for me to approve and the finished pediment arrived about ten days later. Of course, if you have a jigsaw, you could cut out the pediment yourself.

To complement the wardrobe I wanted to find an ornate headboard with attached bedside tables, similar to one my mother has that I have always liked. It took me weeks to find one, but eventually, hidden away behind wardrobes in the back of a junk shop, was the very piece I wanted.

Although the bedhead was Queen Anne style, I was sure that if I painted it in a similar way to the wardrobe the two pieces would blend together well.

CHECKLIST

- Sandpaper in medium and fine grades
- Wet and dry paper
- Traditional paint or emulsion in old white and midnight blue
- Crackle and peel medium
- Artists' acrylic paints in burnt umber, raw sienna, white, grey, Prussian blue, cadmium yellow
- Artists' brushes: in sizes 0 and 1, a long-handled flat size 2 and flat 3 mm (⅛ in)

- Paintbrushes – 25 mm (1 in) and 50 mm (2 in)
- Carbon paper
- Tracing paper and pencil
- Black Bison wax – clear or neutral
- Gilt cream
- Soft lint-free cloth
- Screwdriver
- Four brackets
- Fixing spray

1 DESIGNING AND FIXING THE PEDIMENT TO THE WARDROBE

Measure the distance across the top of the wardrobe and the top sides, and work out the desired height in the middle and at the back of each side. Find a picture or a piece of furniture showing a style you like and draw the shape with the appropriate measurements in the right places, or copy the template provided on page 109. Have the design made into a MDF (medium-density fibreboard) cut-out pediment, or cut it out yourself using a jigsaw. Buy four brackets in the appropriate size so that you can attach the pediment from behind onto the top of the wardrobe. Make sure the edges are flush and screw firmly into place.

2 SANDING THE WARDROBE AND HEADBOARD

Using an electric sander (or by hand), sand off any old waxes or varnish until the surface is smooth enough to paint.

3 PREPARING THE DISTRESSED AREAS

Using the 25 mm (1 in) brush, apply the midnight blue traditional paint, the darker base colour, in patches and strips to the areas where you want a peeled or crackled look. (Take care to avoid the areas where you intend to paint your pattern, so that it does not encroach too much on your design.)

• *Painting on the darker base colour for the distressed areas.*

4 APPLYING THE CRACKLE AND PEEL MEDIUM

Using a 25 mm (1 in) paintbrush, apply the crackle and peel medium over all the areas of midnight blue paint, taking care to avoid runs if possible. If they do occur, sand off lightly once the medium is completely dry.

5 APPLYING THE TOP COAT

With the 50 mm (2 in) paintbrush, apply a generous coat of old white traditional paint to the wardrobe and bedhead. Check that all areas are covered, and use a well-loaded brush on all crackle medium areas to avoid overbrushing. Apply a second, lighter coat of old white paint (but not over the crackled areas), feathering the edges. Some small particles in the crackle area may fall off, but do not worry as this adds to the effect.

• *Applying the burnt umber shading.*

6 APPLYING SHADING

Mix a very watery consistency of burnt umber and, using the larger art brush, paint it around the panels, ornate mouldings, outside edges, inside raised edges and corners of the furniture, to create an aged, shaded effect.

7 ADDING DEPTH

Squeeze a small amount of burnt umber
on to a lid, and shake and open the
midnight blue paint. Using one colour at a
time, dip your thumb and index finger into
the paint and smudge at random along the
top, outside edges, the moulding grooves
and the panel edges. Similarly, run your
thumb around the flat front edges of the
furniture and pediment as well as creating
faint round circles inside the scrolls.

• *Adding depth along the edges.*

8 CREATING AND TRANSFERRING THE DESIGN

Follow the angled lines on the template
on page 107 both as it is and reversed to
create a rounded pattern to fit into the
corners of the curved panels. Use the
whole design horizontally for the bottom
of the panels and the drawers. Draw these
designs onto tracing paper with a heavy
pencil or fine-tip black pen. Place a piece
of carbon paper carbon side down on the
furniture and tape the tracing-paper
pattern on top to hold it in place. Trace
the patterns lightly onto the painted
furniture surface.

9 PAINTING THE DESIGN

Squeeze a small amount of artists' acrylic yellow ochre, cadmium yellow and white onto
a palette and mix well together to create a pale yellow. Then mix grey, Prussian blue and
white to create pale blue-grey. Dip a 3 mm (⅛ in) flat brush into water and side load the
paint, floating it inside the patterns. Use yellow for the flowers and blue for the scrolls.

• *Outlining the edges of the flower patterns
to shade them.*

• *Transferring the design.*

10 SHADING THE EDGES

Using a size 2 round brush with yellow ochre
and burnt sienna, outline the edges of the
flower patterns to shade them. With a size 1
brush use a mixture of grey, Prussian blue
and white to outline the scroll edges. Change
to a size 0 brush to paint the finest lines,
swirls and small details.

• *Using the wet and dry paper to distress the paintwork.*

11 DISTRESSING WITH WET AND DRY PAPER

When the painted patterns are dry, distress the surface very gently by rubbing wet and dry sandpaper up and down over the patterns. Leave some of the design untouched to create an aged look. Sand the rest of the surfaces very lightly, especially the crackled areas, to create a smooth surface for the final waxing.

12 WAXING

Take a soft, clean, lint-free cloth and apply Black Bison wax to the furniture in a gentle circular motion. Leave to dry for at least 20 minutes before buffing to a soft sheen. Dip your thumb and forefinger into the gilt cream and apply it to some of the edges, grooves, scrolls and decorative mouldings. Allow it to dry for 12 hours, then buff to the desired sheen.

• *The distressed paintwork of the finished wardrobe panels.*

• *Applying the finishing gilt cream.*

folding
filigree **screen**

My mother found this wonderful screen at a Sunday morning car boot sale. It had been painted dark brown and did not look very inspiring, but she was amazed at the ridiculously low price the stall holders quoted. She immediately repeated the price with surprise, thinking she must have heard wrongly, but they interpreted this as having priced the screen too high, and made it even cheaper!

I visualized the screen as a real feature in almost any room, painted in a midnight blue colour, and highlighted in gilt wax cream to accentuate the edgings and wonderful cut-out patterns. I thought that it could be further enhanced by adding a small stamped gold star motif around the edging.

When I examined the screen more carefully, I found that there were at least three layers of paint, and as the wood was quite fragile in parts, I felt it would be best just to rub it down gently to remove paint build-up and runs that were present. This also ensured a good painting surface as the old finish was gloss.

The screen looks attractive against plain walls, which emphasize the cut-out patterns, or with vibrant curtains or soft muslin as a backdrop. Standing it in front of a window allows the light to reflect wonderful patterns onto the walls.

$\mathcal{C}$HECKLIST

- Midnight blue acrylic or water-based matt emulsion paint (you can use a spray paint if preferred)
- Motif stamp
- Stamp roller or art brush
- Gold watercolour paint or craft paint
- Saucer or small container
- Gilt cream
- Spray polyurethane varnish in satin finish
- Art brush – size 8
- Paintbrush – 40 mm (1½ in)
- Sandpaper in medium and fine grades

▌ PREPARATION

Rub down the screen with medium and then fine sandpaper to remove all paint build-ups and flaking paint. Wipe down with a dry cloth and then clean the screen with warm soapy water, using an old toothbrush to get into the corners and patterns. Allow to dry thoroughly.

• *A detail showing the gold stars and gilt highlights.*

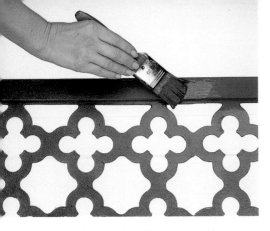

• *Applying midnight blue paint to the screen.*

2 PAINTING THE SCREEN

Cover the floor with a plastic sheet or newspaper and paint the entire screen with two coats of midnight blue paint, using an art brush to paint into the crevices and cut-out patterns. Allow to dry between coats. You may find it easier to paint the screen with it lying flat. You can also use a spray paint to cover the screen if preferred, but this should be done outside or in a well-ventilated area.

3 POSITIONING THE MOTIF

Measure the frame surrounds of one entire section and divide this equally to space out the gold star stamp pattern. As all three panels are the same you will only have to work this out once.

4 STAMPING THE MOTIF ONTO THE SCREEN

Lay the screen flat before starting to apply the motif. Pour a small amount of gold paint into a dish. Work paint into the roller until it is coated with paint, then roll this over the stamp. Simply press the stamp in position and remove using one swift action. If you do not have a stamp roller, and you have purchased your stamp in an art shop or stationer's, simply dip an

• *Stamping the motif.*

art brush into the gold paint and apply a coat of this to the stamp. If you wish to have a very definite motif you need to re-coat with paint after each application. If you prefer a faded look, then re-coat when necessary.

5 HIGHLIGHTING EDGES

Apply a small amount of gilt cream to your thumb and forefinger and smudge it into all cut-outs and edges. Leave to dry and buff gently to a soft sheen.

6 VARNISH FINISH

Spray the screen evenly with one coat of satin varnish and allow to dry thoroughly before use.

• *Applying gilt cream to the edges of the cut-outs.*

MAKING YOUR OWN STAMP MOTIF

*C*HECKLIST
• Scalpel and blade
• Fine marker
• Pen
• A cork or a potato

You can buy many stamps now to apply patterns and motifs from companies who produce kits, and if you cannot find a suitable design some of them will make one for you. You can also buy stamps in art and decorating stores, with a choice of colours and as whole kits with instructions.

If you want to make your own stamp very cheaply, however, here is how.

1 Creating your design

Draw your design on the flat side of the cork or potato – the inside of the pattern will be the raised part.

2 Cutting out the design

Cut with the scalpel around the outside of the pattern markings. Try the stamp out and alter it until you are happy with the result, then proceed to use as directed in the steps for stamping the screen.

gilt stencilled mirror

• *Detail of gold-painted cherubs that can be added to the top of the mirror.*

This large old mirror measures approximately 1.8 x 1.5 m (6 x 5 ft). The frame was old gold and dirty, with parts of it missing. It was hanging on the wall in a derelict old mews house that a friend of mine had purchased. Unable to see its potential, he gladly passed it on to me when I expressed an interest. On seeing the result he has jokingly stated that he regrets his decision. The mirror is now one of the talking points of my home.

𝒞HECKLIST

• Eggshell paint for base coat
• Small tin of scumble glaze (or paint effect glaze)
• Clean cotton cloth
• Sheet of plastic stencil film
• Scalpel
• Gold crayon stencil stick
• Gold paint
• Black universal stainer
• Brushes
• Fine sandpaper
• White spirit
• Stencil brush – small
• Small flat size 2 art brush
• Spray adhesive

1 PREPARING THE FRAME

Clean the frame with a weak sugar soap solution and fill in cracks or holes with standard filler. Rub the frame down with fine sandpaper to ensure a smooth surface for painting.

2 BASE COAT

Choose a base colour (I used white eggshell with a few drops of black universal stainer to make pale grey) and paint on two good coats of eggshell.

3 MIXING GLAZE AND RAGGING

Mix up a small amount of scumble glaze, using 3 parts scumble to 1 part white spirit. Add a few drops of black universal stainer and a small amount of grey eggshell basecoat and stir well. Paint the mixture onto the frame and dab immediately with a scrunched rag or plastic carrier bag to give a rag-roll effect.

4 MAKING THE STENCIL

Trace a small fleur de lys and star design onto paper (see page 107), then transfer it onto the matt side of the stencil film. Cut out the designs with a scalpel blade. (Or buy your stencil from a selection in stencil shops.)

• *Cutting out the stencil design.*

5 STENCILLING ONTO THE FRAME

Stencil the two designs onto the frame at regular intervals using the gold wax crayon and following the manufacturer's instructions on the pack.

• *Applying the stencil onto the frame with a gold wax crayon.*

• *Painting the outer gold rim.*

6 FINISHING

Paint a fine gold line around the outside of the frame using gold varnish paint.

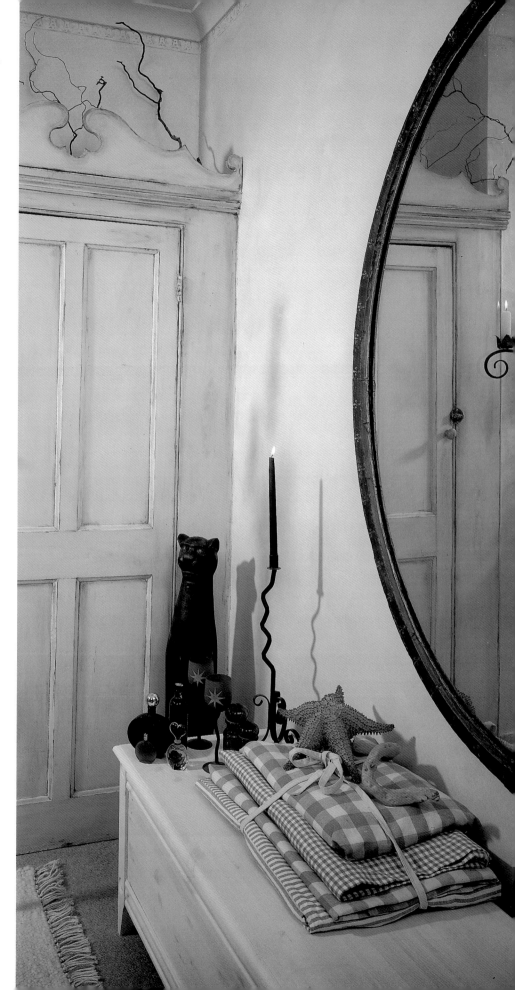

carved
linen cupboard

This cupboard was sitting in a junk shop for some time and parts of the door frame were missing. Eventually the price went down, so I examined it more carefully and it was obvious that a half-hearted attempt had been made to start cleaning it up and stripping down the wood. I pulled out a drawer to see if the back of it was made of the same wood as the broken door, as I knew I could use this to replace the missing parts. When I discovered this was so, I made an offer and took the piece home.

My friend Jane, who had just finished a degree that included furniture restoration, made the missing pieces. If you do not have a contact who can do this, you can find a carpenter in a business directory.

I set about bringing the cupboard back to its natural sheen and beauty – it turned out to be made from three different kinds of wood, some containing straight grain, others with a smooth finish. I decided to use liming wax to enhance the beautiful carved panels and edgings and set about getting the dirt and old wax out of the carved areas. A rub with fine wire wool was sufficient to brighten up the hinges.

𝒞HECKLIST

- Liming wax
- Cream and neutral furniture wax
- Electric sander with/or sandpaper in medium and fine grades
- Tack cloth
- Clean lint-free cloth
- Wire brush
- Art brush – size 4
- Long-handled fitch brush

▌ SANDING

Using the electric sander and medium-grade sandpaper, place the sander on the chest and sand with a forward and back motion following the grain of the wood; if you use a circular motion across the grain you will damage the wood surface. When the surface dirt and old finish has been removed, change to fine sandpaper and repeat the process until the surface is smooth to the touch.

• *Sanding down the chest with an electric sander.*

• *Opening up the grain of the wood.*

• *Applying liming wax with an art brush.*

• *Removing the excess wax.*

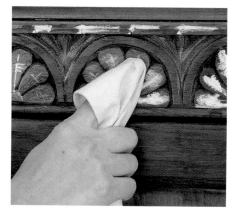

2 OPENING UP THE GRAIN

Open up the grain on the carved pieces by using a one-way sweeping motion with the wire brush in the direction of the grain, as this enables the liming wax to penetrate into the wood. Wipe down thoroughly to remove any dust.

3 APPLYING THE LIMING WAX

Because of the intricate pattern I am not using the normal method of working liming wax on with a cloth. Instead, dip an art brush into the liming wax and paint it into and all over the carved areas, especially into the grooves and carvings. Leave for only ten minutes before going on to the next step.

4 REMOVING EXCESS WAX

With the clean lint-free cloth, wipe off the excess liming wax on the flat surface areas of the raised patterns, but leave the build-up of wax in the grooves, pattern niches and edges as this creates the limed effect. Leave to harden thoroughly overnight.

5 WAX AND BUFF THE LIMED AREAS

Using a wad of clean soft cloth, rub this into the neutral wax and apply over the limed areas. Leave the wax for approximately 20 minutes and then buff to a sheen with a clean lint-free cloth. If the limed areas look too white against the natural tones of the chest, repeat the waxing with neutral polish as this will tone it down and create a more aged effect.

6 WAXING THE REMAINING WOOD

Apply cream wax over the rest of the cupboard and leave to soak into the wood for at least an hour and then gently buff to a sheen finish. This process needs to be repeated over a period of time to obtain a really good finish. Try not to infringe on the ornate areas with the cream wax as this will create a yellowing effect which you do not want.

• *A detail showing how the liming wax enhances the grain of the wood.*

cherub wardrobe

This type of wardrobe is very inexpensive and can be readily obtained from junk shops. It was originally a gentleman's wardrobe, but modern children's wardrobes are made to a similar design. The one I have purchased is of good solid wood, with shelving up one side and a hanging rail, which makes it ideal for a child or for a small guest room.

You need flat doors so that the stencil can be applied to best effect. I used a rag-rolling technique and you will find the cherub stencil on page 110. I have designed a two-piece cherub stencil – one overlays the other – and this creates a shaded effect, giving the finished picture depth and features. This means that you need to apply a light colour first and then use a darker shade for the overlay. When you are actually stencilling, you may feel that you have not applied enough paint, but this is the right effect as when you remove the stencil it will be much heavier than you imagine. An overloaded brush and heavy paint cause smudging and do not produce the soft texture that stencilling requires.

To add that final finishing touch, I purchased two silver tassels from a soft-furnishing department of a store. If your handles are not suitable for painting, or do not blend in with the wardrobe, you can purchase glass or silver knobs or handles that really enhance the appearance.

CHECKLIST

- Stencil film and permanent pen
- Cherub stencil (see page 110)
- Black and white stencil sticks
- Medium-sized stencil brush
- Transparent oil glaze or acrylic (you can buy ready-made acrylic mixes)
- White spirit
- Clean lint-free cotton rags
- Radiator roller with sleeve for oil-based paint
- Stipple brush
- Eggshell base coat (I used a pink colour)
- Tape measure
- Spray mount
- Two silver tassels
- Two glass knobs
- Paint tray
- Paint brush – 50 mm (2 in)
- Sander with/or sandpaper in medium and fine grades
- Primer

1 PREPARATION

Sand down the entire surface of the wardrobe using a sander or sandpaper following the grain of the wood. Wipe down with a damp cloth and allow to dry. Remove old handles if possible as it will make the piece easier to paint. If changing the handles, fill in any obsolete holes at this stage.

2 PAINTING THE BASE COAT

Apply a coat of primer first, then, using the radiator roller with a sleeve for oil-based paint, pour the eggshell paint into the tray and apply it to the entire cupboard. Touch up edgings if required with a small paintbrush. Leave to dry for the manufacturer's recommended time and then apply a second coat. If there are any runs or paint build-up you can sand with fine sandpaper between coats.

• *Applying eggshell paint with a radiator roller.*

• *Using a stippling brush over the glaze.*

3 MIXING THE GLAZE

Place a spoon of transparent oil glaze into the paint kettle, and squeeze into it a tube width of black artists' oil paint; stir this into the glaze until smooth. Continue adding more transparent oil glaze plus white spirit in the ratio of two parts glaze to one part of white spirit, finally adding one spoon of pink flesh-tone eggshell, until you have a sufficient quantity for your project. The stirring consistency should be that of single cream. (I used eight spoons of glaze for this project – it is better to have too much rather than too little.)

4 APPLYING THE GLAZE AND CREATING THE STIPPLING EFFECT

Dip the 50 mm (2 in) brush into the glaze, and with a well-loaded brush paint one complete section of the wardrobe at a time, working quickly and not overbrushing. Do not allow the glaze to dry but with the stippling brush use a moderate up and down stabbing motion to remove the brush strokes, to create a fine speckle-effect finish. If you do not have a stippling brush place a clean sleeve for oil-based paint on the radiator roller and very gently roll over the glaze to smooth out the brush strokes. Continue onto the next step immediately you have done this.

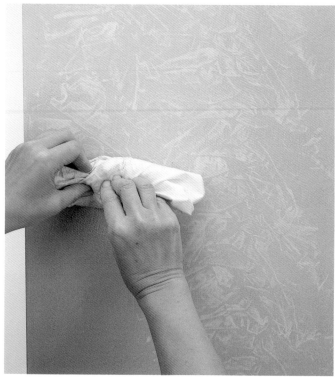

• *Rag rolling down the glaze.*

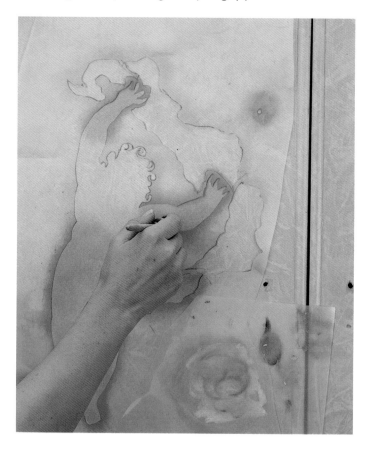

7 STENCILLING THE CHERUB — PART 1

Measure the middle of the wardrobe and, spacing away from the door handles, apply spray adhesive to the wrong side of Part 1 stencil and stick it into place on the wardrobe door. Stand back and see if it is in the right position and adjust if necessary. Break the seals of the stencil sticks (instructions are given on them). Working an amount of black and white onto the spare area of the film that was allowed for this purpose, mix together until you have a pale grey shade. Working the stencil brush into this mix cover all cut-out areas of Part 1, using a circular and stippling motion. You need to paint the positioning marks as well. Carefully peel off the stencil.

• *Stencilling Part 1 of the design with pale grey paint.*

5 RAG ROLLING

Cut up the cotton material into large rag pieces. Screw up a piece of rag and then twist it into a sausage shape. Place the rag at a top corner and roll the rag down to the bottom of the wardrobe using your fingertips and applying pressure. Continue this process, very slightly overlapping onto your last pattern to avoid hard edges. Leave at least 24 hours to dry.

6 MAKING THE CHERUB STENCIL

Allow a surplus of plastic stencil film around the edges to mix colours, and for the positioning marks. Place the film over the template for Part 1 of the cherub stencil on page 110 and trace the outline onto the sheet with a fine-tip permanent pen. Cut along the lines with a scalpel and cut out the circular line-up dots, which will enable you to position the second stencil cut-out in the correct place. On a separate piece of film repeat the same for Part 2 of the stencil.

8 STENCILLING THE CHERUB — PART 2

Spray and place Part 2 on the wardrobe, aligning the position marks. Mix the stencil sticks as before but create a dark grey colour, and keep some neat black beside this to highlight small areas. Colour all the cut-out areas with dark grey, accentuating some small parts and features by stippling with a small amount of black. Peel the stencil off.

Wipe off the line-up dots. Clean the stencil with a clean rag and white spirit and allow to dry. Repeat the process on the other door by reversing the stencil and again following the Part 1 and Part 2 instructions. Wipe off the line-up dots.

Leave at least 24 hours to dry thoroughly.

9 APPLYING THE ACRYLIC GLAZE

With the acrylic brush, finish the wardrobe by applying two coats of acrylic satin glaze. This initially gives the appearance of a milky finish but it will dry clear, so do not overwork as the glaze dries very quickly. Allow the manufacturer's recommended drying time between coats.

• *Stencilling Part 2 of the design with dark grey paint.*

• *Detail showing the darker stencilled parts of the cherub.*

• *Detail of the finished painted cherub.*

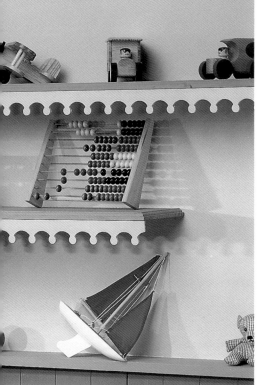

toy soldier
bedstead

I decided to decorate a child's bedhead with découpage, to demonstrate that you can use any pictures for doing this, not just the usual roses and old-fashioned cut-outs. I spent some time looking for a suitably shaped headboard, and was excited to find this quite old, curved one, which was part of a complete bed. The shape of the bedhead inspired me to illustrate the 'Grand Old Duke of York' nursery rhyme, because the soldiers could literally march up the hill and down the hill again.

I asked my friend Christine, a piano teacher, to write some music notes by hand. My father paints watercolours and spent an enjoyable afternoon with my daughter drawing and painting soldiers. I took the soldiers to a colour photocopy shop, enlarged and copied the first four, and then continued until I had an army to cut out. I photocopied the sheet music onto cream paper.

Pick a really bright base colour for your bedhead as the découpage needs several coats of varnish, which tends to yellow the colour down.

Checklist

- Furniture cleaner
- Sheet music
- Craft glue and brush
- Varnish – acrylic or oil
- Varnish brush
- Blu-tack
- Acrylic eggshell or emulsion base coat paint
- Paintbrushes
- Small craft scissors
- Tea bag
- Soft clean cloth
- Sanding sealer/primer

(All paints and varnishes can be purchased as non-toxic especially for use for young children's furniture.)

• *Applying the base coat of paint.*

1 PREPARATION

Rub down the headboard and clean with furniture cleaner to remove old varnish and dirt from the surface. Rub down with a dry cloth when dry and apply a coat of sanding sealer.

2 PAINTING THE BASE COAT

Paint two coats of paint over the headboard and legs (if any), allowing the manufacturer's recommended drying time between coats. Paint a rim of bright red around the outside edge moulding.

3 COPYING THE CUT-OUTS

Draw or paint toy soldiers onto white paper; photocopy (using a colour photocopier) as many as possible onto one sheet, and then repeat photocopying until you have sufficient for your army. Alternatively, collect pictures of soldiers. Copy or obtain pieces of music and copy onto cream paper or use original music.

• *Cutting out the paper toy soldiers.*

4 CUTTING THE PICTURES

Carefully cut out the soldiers, the central horseman and an assortment of drummers, riflemen and further horsemen. With a sweeping motion using the scissors round off the edges of the music to make them look like old manuscripts.

5 AGEING THE MUSIC

Wipe a wet, warm, intact tea bag round the edges of the sheets of music and across them in places to create an old, well-used appearance. Leave the paper to dry thoroughly.

• *Wiping the edges of the sheet music with a tea bag.*

• *Planning the positions of the soldiers using Blu-tack.*

• *Pasting the soldiers into position.*

6 POSITIONING THE DESIGN

It is advisable to position the figures and music in place using Blu-tack, then stand back and view the whole picture. Sometimes a picture looks perfect close up, but when you stand back to get an overall view angles may not be right, and some pieces may need repositioning. Remember to take into account the width of the mattress and pillows, otherwise you may hide a great deal of your picture when the bed is made up.

When you are happy with the overall effect, paste the back of the figures with glue, making sure you cover all the edges. Place them into position and smooth down with a clean cloth, removing any excess glue immediately. Leave to dry.

7 VARNISHING

Traditional découpage has approximately a dozen coats of varnish applied until the

• *Varnishing the découpage.*

paper and paint levels are smooth to the touch. The headboard will need at least three coats with a good clear varnish to make sure they are secure and well

covered, but if you wish you can apply further coats. Leave the manufacturer's recommended drying time between coats.

mosaic
terracotta **vase**

bought this terracotta vase in a charity shop as it looked a good shape to transform into a tall unusual container for large natural flower arrangements and long-stemmed flowers. I saw the small plaster cherubs in an interior decorative plaster shop on the way home and thought they would add an interesting touch, and planned to verdigris these. You can buy these already with a verdigris finish or gold finish from shops, garden centres, markets and Christmas stalls. Other decorative plaster pieces are also available.

I had a small sheet of mosaic in my studio and chose glass coloured shapes to combine with the mosaic. Mosaic tile sheets can be bought from tile stockists and there are mail order companies who specialize in mosaic and mosaic patterns, or you could use any tile or ceramic pieces broken up. As you only need a small amount of mosaic you could probably find the end of a range at quite a low price.

• Gluing the cherubs around the vase.

First you need an idea of what you wish to create, and then you can collect the decorative pieces you are going to use. You could use Blu-tack to place them in position to see what they will look like.

Use an all-in-one mixture to fix and grout. When using grout on any tiling projects, always wipe off the excess immediately from the surface of the tile, or if you need to reposition any, do this immediately before it begins to dry, as it is difficult to remove after drying. If you wish to cut up tiles you can buy an inexpensive hand tile-cutter from any DIY store.

*C*HECKLIST
- Damp cloth or sponge
- PVA waterproof or tile adhesive
- Tile-cutters
- Grouting
- 4 plaster verdigris cherubs (see page 39)
- Sheet of mosaic tiles
- Glass decorative shapes

❙ SECURING THE DECORATIVE PIECES

Make sure all surfaces are clean, sound and free of dust. Then, using PVA adhesive and sealer, stick the four cherubs equally spaced around the top rim of the vase.

• *Cutting the mosaic pieces.*

2 PREPARATION FOR THE MOSAIC

It looks more effective to create curves and diagonals with your mosaic pieces. Use tile-cutters to make triangles, small oblongs and pieces to fit around the cherubs and between other gaps created by your pattern, as shown in the photograph.

• *Fixing the mosaics in position on the vase.*

3 FIX AND GROUT METHOD

Coat a small area of the vase with fix and grout. Place the mosaic pieces into position as described above, making sure grout is in the small gaps between the pieces and wipe down the surface with a damp cloth or sponge to remove any excess. Continue in this way until the vase sides are covered. Allow the manufacturer's recommended time to dry.

4 FINISHING OFF

Using PVA adhesive, stick the decorative glass shapes into place around the top rim of the vase and leave to dry. Buff the mosaic with a clean lint-free cloth.

• *Using a damp sponge to fill the gaps between mosaics with grout.*

calligraphy lampshades

A lampshade can be transformed very simply, just by using a gold metallic art pen, a skein of garden raffia and a stick of sealing wax to give a finishing touch. My inspiration for this project came from the many fabric and china designs that have appeared recently featuring gold calligraphy in many languages. I obtained these lampshades at a garage sale and they were perfect for my tall, black, wrought-iron bedside lamps. This was the first time I had tried out this idea; I was happy with my first attempt and the lampshades are now in use.

There are many books on calligraphy and if you are visiting a museum it is worthwhile looking at old books, scrolls and wall hangings to obtain different ideas. A foreign dictionary often has a section with well-known phrases that you can also use for an authentic touch. If you have not attempted calligraphy before, you would be wise to practise before writing directly onto your lampshade.

For the sealing stamps I bought a stick of sealing wax from a stationery shop, but kits of personalized sealing stamps with sealing wax are available. I used an old Italian coin glued onto a heavy bolthead to create my own stamp and detached it later. Many antique stalls sell old sealing stamps, some of which have very interesting designs.

$\mathcal{C}$HECKLIST

- A can of decorative gold spray
- Fine-tip gold flow metallic art pen
- Ball of raffia (can be obtained at garden centres)
- Craft glue or glue gun
- Piece of artists' mounting card
- Scalpel
- Wax sealing stick and stamp

1 SPRAY INSIDE OF LAMPSHADE

Spray the inside of the lampshade with the gold decorative spray, taking care not to get it onto the right side, and leave to dry thoroughly. You need to lay down paper or a sheet of plastic to protect the surroundings, and you need to ventilate the room or spray outside if possible.

2 CALLIGRAPHY

When you have found the words you want to write and style of calligraphy to use, practise using the gold flowing art pen and applying the writing onto the piece of artists' card in sentences and broken patterns. This will give you the opportunity of planning their position on the lampshade, and deciding what angles to use. The pen needs to be shaken vigorously (make sure you are pointing it at the protected surface while doing this) and then push in the point on the card until the gold starts to flow. This procedure needs to be repeated when the natural flow slows down.

• *Applying the calligraphy to the lampshade with a gold metallic pen.*

3 WRITING ON THE SHADE

Now you have chosen the writing patterns and styles you wish to apply, shake the pen as in step two and carefully write onto the shade itself. I think it looks quite effective to shake the pen so that gold spatters onto the shade.

• *Applying the seal on a piece of card.*

4 PREPARING THE RAFFIA

Cut six lengths of raffia approximately twice the circumference of the bottom of the shade. Secure one set of ends and neatly plait three double strands to fit around the bottom rim allowing some overlap (as shown in the photograph). Glue the plait round the bottom of the shade, but fray off the ends; stick down one set of ends and overlap the other, leaving approximately 3 cm (1¼ in) unplaited and frayed. Repeat the process for the top rim of the shade but exclude the overlap piece, simply cutting and sticking down the ends to make a neat join. If you do not obtain a neat join you could place a second seal as camouflage.

5 APPLYING THE SEAL

Melt the sealing wax onto the card by lighting the wick end and allowing the wax to drip. Quickly press the stamp in and out while it is hot. This will set quickly and you can cut around the card close to the seal with a scalpel blade — leaving the card attached will prevent the seal from cracking. Glue into position over the join of the raffia as shown. By applying the sealing wax to the card you will also eliminate any damage to your shade if the technique goes wrong.

• *Plaiting the raffia trimming.*

• *Sticking the raffia trimming around the top of the lampshade.*

malachite
painted **box**

Small wooden boxes are quite easy to find at a reasonable cost; I have found several in junk shops and car boot sales. Often gifts such as wine and cigars are packed in wooden boxes that can be totally transformed. I found the box in this project at a car boot sale, where an old gentleman had made up all his odd pieces of wood into boxes and was selling them at a very low price. The wood is good quality, and the box is well made, but the edges and joins were rough to the touch, and no finish had been applied, so it was ideal for transforming from its raw state into a beautiful item.

I have often found small items like wooden boxes while searching for other larger items. If they have a bad finish, or are a little damaged, it is worthwhile looking at them closely to decide whether you can strip back to natural wood and repair the box.

Boxes can be finished in many ways, such as by applying stencilling, hand-painted designs, découpage, paint techniques and distressing. I have always thought that malachite was a beautiful stone, and decided to decorate a personalized box to give to a friend for a special occasion. The gesso coat that is applied initially infills the wood grain and allows the creation of a wonderful sheen finish simulating a polished-stone effect.

Gesso is used as a preparation before water gilding, and also for painted furniture when a fine finish is required. It is made from rabbit skin size and gilders' whiting. Used on unpainted surfaces, gesso fills the grain of wood and can be rubbed down to a fine smooth finish. Although this technique requires many coats of different mediums and much patience, the end result is well worth it.

$\mathcal{C}$HECKLIST

- Oil-based eggshell paint – pale sea green
- Transparent oil glaze
- Tubes of artists' oil pigment – viridian and burnt sienna
- Raw linseed oil, white spirit and liquid dryers (this makes the gilp – with 1 part oil, 2 parts white spirit and 5 drops of dryers)
- Straightedge
- Clean rag
- Fine glasspaper
- Small brush

Materials for making gesso:
- Rabbit skin size
- Gilders' whiting
- Sieve
- Saucepan
- Pot that fits into the saucepan
- Soft brush or mop for application of gesso

❚ PREPARING THE BOX

If possible, take the lid and the hinges off the box so that it is easier to create the malachite finish evenly on all edges. If your box has a lock, you may be able to remove this, too. Thoroughly rub down the surfaces with glasspaper and wipe with a soft dry cloth to remove any particles of sawdust.

2 MAKING THE GESSO

The recipe for gesso is 1 part rabbit skin size to 16 parts water (by volume). Whiting is added later.

Place the size in a suitable container with 6 parts of water. Let this stand for two hours to soften. Add the remaining water, then place the pot in a saucepan of hot water on a low heat until melted. Take off the heat, retain a small amount of size to use in step 3 and then sieve gilders' whiting into the remaining warm size. Keep adding whiting until it is about 6 mm (¼ in) below the surface of the size, and gently stir (the consistency should be the thickness of single cream). Leave in the fridge overnight as this allows trapped air in the gesso to escape.

3 APPLYING GESSO

Using a brush, apply the size to the surface made to the original 1:16 mixture that you have reserved without the addition of whiting. Allow to dry overnight. Warm the gesso in a saucepan of hot water on a low heat to blood heat. Using a soft brush, apply a coat of gesso in quick, straight, brush strokes. Look along the surface and, as soon as the sheen has disappeared, apply the next coat by stippling on with the soft brush, still keeping the gesso at blood heat. Apply more coats as the sheen disappears, stippling

• *Rubbing down the dried gesso surface on the box.*

every other coat until you have applied at least five coats. Allow to dry for 24 hours.

Carefully rub down the surfaces with fine glasspaper to a smooth finish – this makes a mess, so do it somewhere that is easy to clean and away from where you are going to do any painting.

4 SEALING THE GESSO SURFACES

Apply a coat of sealer or primer with a mixture of varnish (part by volume), white spirit (part by volume) and raw linseed oil (one half-part by volume). Allow to dry overnight.

• *Applying the gesso in quick, straight brush strokes.*

5 DENIB THE BASE COAT

'Denib' all surfaces (lightly rub down with
fine glasspaper). Apply at least two coats
of oil-based pale sea-green eggshell paint,
allowing to dry overnight between each.
You need to lightly rub down the surface
with fine glasspaper between coats.

6 PLANNING THE MALACHITE PATTERNS

Using a pencil and a small straightedge,
mark out irregular sections covering each
surface of the box.

7 MIXING THE COLOUR

Mix a rich green colour, using transparent
oil glaze and viridian pigment, with just a
touch of burnt sienna to sage the green
slightly to stop it being too blue. Make the
gilp with 1 part oil, 2 parts white spirit and
5 drops of dryers. Then thin the glaze
slightly with the gilp.

• *Applying oil-based pale sea-green eggshell paint to the box.*

• *Using a straightedge to draw irregular shapes on the box.*

• *Using card to emulate the look of malachite.*

• *Defining the edges of the shapes by wiping with a clean rag.*

8 APPLYING THE GLAZE

Using a paintbrush, apply glaze to alternate sections that have no adjoining edges. Take a piece of stiff card and, using a straightedge, tear off a piece slightly larger than the section marked. Drag this piece of card through the glaze with a shaky movement to emulate the lines and swirls that are so characteristic of malachite. Vary the direction of each separate section when dragging through the glaze to create a realistic effect of malachite stone. Use a straightedge and clean rag to wipe the excess glaze back to the drawn shape. Let the glaze dry thoroughly overnight.

The following day continue to fill in the remaining shapes, wiping back the excess glaze as before. Allow to dry overnight. Continue creating the malachite patterns until all the sections have been filled in.

9 FINISHING WITH VARNISH

Wipe the box with a clean, dry cloth. Apply a coat of gloss varnish; allow it to dry overnight and then gently rub the surface with a fine finishing glasspaper. Repeat these steps until you have a high gloss finish. This may take

• *Applying varnish to the painted box.*

several costs of varnish. DO NOT RUB DOWN THE FINAL COAT. You must make sure you allow the manufacturer's recommended drying time between coats.

10 FINISHING THE INSIDE OF THE BOX

The inside of the box can be painted or lined with a fabric of your choice.

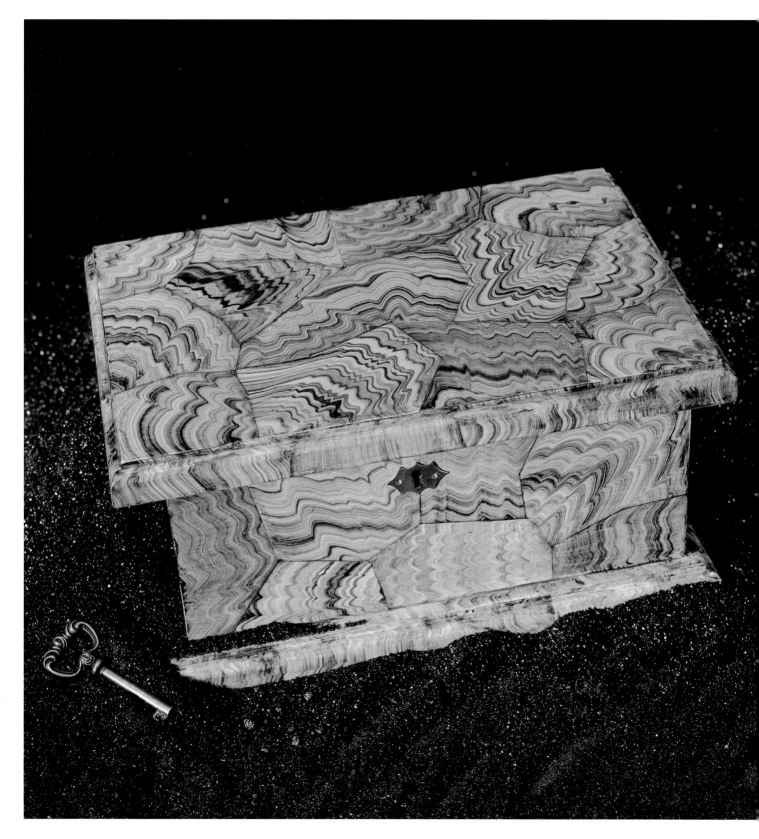

templates

• *Glass-fronted cupboard*

• *Glass-fronted cupboard*

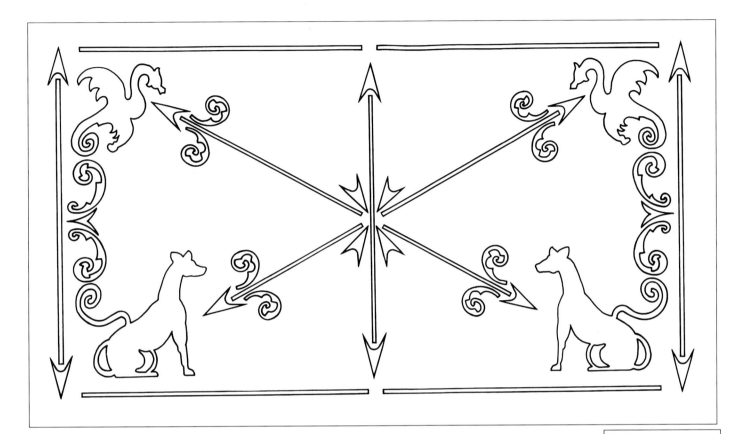

• *Heraldic writing desk.*

• *Scandinavian style scroll chair & Wardrobe and headboard*

• *Decanter and glasses*
& Gilt stencilled mirror

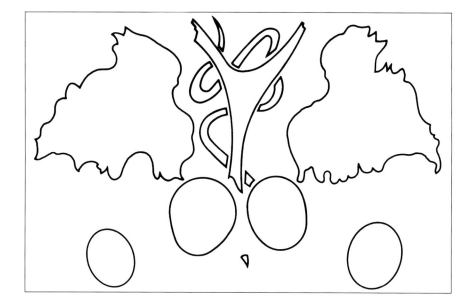

• *Vine leaf table*

• *Vine leaf table*

• *Bathroom cupboard*

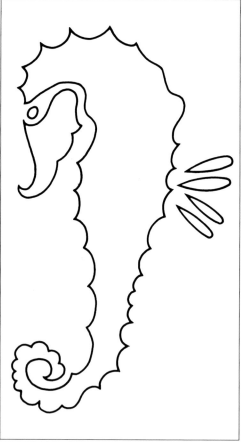

• *Bathroom cupboard*

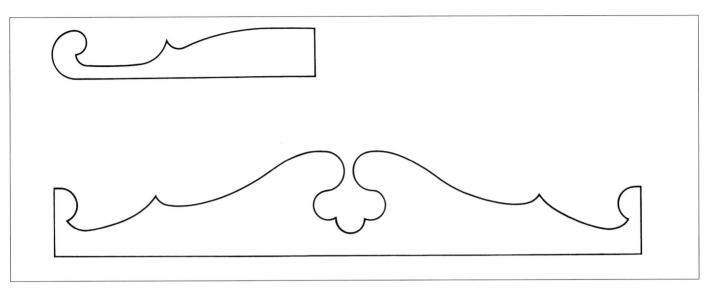

• *Wardrobe and headboard (scroll style pediment)*

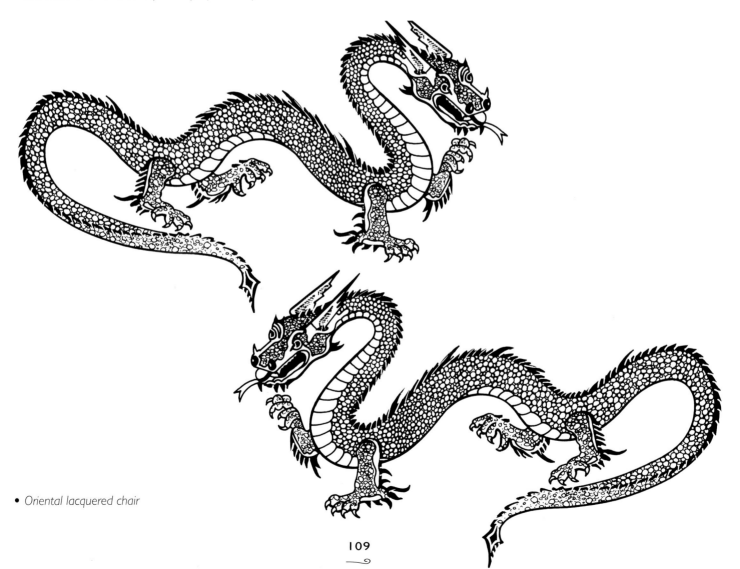

• *Oriental lacquered chair*

• *Cherub wardrobe Part 1*

• *Cherub wardrobe Part 2*

• *Oriental lacquered chair*

suppliers

Bloemfontein

L & P Stationery and Artists'
Requirements
65b Church Street
Tel: (051) 30-3061

L & P Stationery and Artists'
Requirements
141a Zastron Street
Tel: (051) 30-1085

Mycrafts Arts and Crafts Shop
Aliwal Street
Tel: (051) 48-4119

Wardkiss Homecare
Cor. Zastron Street and
Second Ave
Westdene
Tel: (051) 47-6881

Cape Town

Anne's Arts and Crafts
6 Recreation Road
Fishoek
Tel: (021) 782-2061

Colorwall (Pty.) Ltd.
79 Long Street
Tel: (021) 23-2434

Crafty Suppliers
32 Main Road
Claremont
Tel: (021) 61-0286

The Deckle Edge
Southern Riverside Centre
Rondebosch
Tel: (021) 685-1950

Est Graphics
59 Shortmarket Street
Tel: (021) 23-4365

In-fin-art
9 Wolfe Street, Wineberg
Tel: (021) 761-2816

Paper Paradise
Paradyspark Shopping Centre
Brackenfell
Tel: (021) 982-4222

Le Papier du Port
Gardens Centre
Tel: (021) 462-4796
Mail orders: PO Box 50055
Waterfront 8002

Papyrus
Sanlam Centre
Parow
Tel: (021) 930-4031

Peers Handicrafts
35 Burg Street
Tel: (021) 24-2520
Fax: 23-9646
Mail orders: PO Box 912, Cape
Town 8000

Wardkiss Homecare
Blue Route Centre, Tokai, Tel:
(021) 72-5000
Mill Street, Gardens
Tel: (021) 461-7202
Rosmead Avenue, Kenilworth,
Tel: (021) 683-3610
Voortrekker Road,
Goodwood
Tel: (021) 591-9144

Durban

Art, Leather and Handcraft
Specialists
Musgrave Centre
Tel: (031) 21-9517

Art Mates
Musgrave Centre
Tel: (031) 21-0094

Bishop Merchandising
Company
89 Russel Street
Tel: (031) 301-4737

PW Story (Pty) Ltd
18 Foundry Ave
Tel: (031) 306-1224

Wardkiss Homecare
Sydney Road
Tel: (031) 25-1551

Argyle Road
Tel: (031) 309-5485

East London

Burmeisters
Cor Fleet- & Signal Streets
Tel: (0431) 2-4272

Cottage Craft
20 Pearce Street, Berea
Tel: (0431) 57-231

Federated Timbers
39 Commercial Road
Tel: (0431) 43-3733

George

Art, Craft & Hobbies
72 Hibernia Street
Tel: (0441) 74-1337

The Art Shop
Tommy Joubert Plaza
Market Street
Tel: (0441) 73-2792

Johannesburg

Action DIY Centre
27 Madison Street, Jeppe
Tel: (011) 614-1700
East Rand Tower Shopping
Centre, Boksburg
Tel: (011)823-5555

Avies Arts & Crafts
26 Rocky Street
Bellevue
Tel: (011)648-7009

The Craftsman
Progress House
110 Bordeaux Drive
Randburg
Tel: (011) 787-1846

Effective Visual Expression
Millpark Gallery
Aucklandpark
Tel: (011) 482-1467

Southern Arts & Crafts
105 Main Street, Rosettenville
Tel: (011) 683-6566

Newcastle

Polka Dot
Voortrekker Road
Tel: (03431) 29-792

Wardkiss Homecare
20 Scott Street
Tel: (03431) 26-187

Pietermaritzburg

The Art Shop
197 Longmarket Street
Perks' Arcade
Tel: (0331) 94-7917

PW Story (Pty) Ltd
Cascades Centre
Mc Carthy Drive
Montrose
Tel: (0331) 45-3994

Wardkiss Homecare
223 Pietermaritzburg Street
Tel: (0331) 45-4315

Port Elizabeth

Corner Arts and Crafts
63 Fourth Ave
Newtonpark
Tel: (041) 35-2487
Westborne Road 68
Tel: (041) 33-1824

Pretoria

E. Schweikerdt (Pty.) Ltd.
Vatika Centre
Cor. Muckleneuk & Fehrsen
Streets
Brooklyn
Tel: (012) 45-5406
590 Souter Street
Pretoria West
Tel: (012)327-0708/9
Mail orders: PO Box 697,
Pretoria, 0001

Franken
445 Hilda Street 445
Hatfield
Tel: (012) 43-6414

index

acrylic glazes 17, 63, 91
acrylic paint, artists' 17
acrylic varnishes 17
  brushes 17
ageing effects 53, 67, 94

Black Bison wax 18
Blu-tack 18
broken colour 18
brushes
  acrylic 17
  artists' 18
  cleaners 19
  dragging 20
  fitch 20
  general purpose 20
  lacquer 21
  paint 22
  restorers 19
  softener 24
  stencil 25
  stippling 25
burnishing 55

carbon paper 19
china filler 19
church fittings dealers 11
clingfilm effects 61
cracked wood 12
crackle and peel medium 19, 30,
49, 52, 76
crackle varnish 19, 67

découpage 19
designs
  creating 36
  painting 36, 77
  tracing 49
  see also stencils
distressing 76, 78
dragging 35
  brushes 20
dry rot 12
dry wood 12

fillers, wood 27
finishes
  ageing 53, 67, 94

broken colour 18
crackle and peel medium 19, 30,
49, 52, 76
crackle varnish 19, 67
distressing 76, 78
dragging 20, 35
glitter glue 44
granite effect 37–8
lacquer 21, 55
liming wax 21, 86
malachite effect 101–5
rag rolling 82, 90
stippling 25, 88
verdigris 39–41
wax 32, 50, 53, 57, 77
  see also glazes; paint; varnishes
fitch brushes 20
fixing spray 20
Formica, painting 14

gesso 20, 102
gilp 20
gilt cream 21, 50
glass
  paint 21
  stencilling 72
glasspapers 24
glazes
  acrylic 17, 63, 91
  applying 35, 104
  granite effect 38
  mixing 35, 88
  scumble 26
  transparent oil 26
glitter glue 44
glue
  glitter 44
  rabbit skin 23, 66

lacquer
  brushes 21
  finishes 55
light fittings 15
liming wax 21, 86

MDF 22
melamine, painting 14

oil glazes, transparent 26
oil paint, artists' 18
oil-based paint 22
oil-based varnish 22

paint
  acrylic 17, 26
  glass 21, 45
  kettles 22
  oil, 18
  oil-based 22
  palettes 22
  primers 23
  spray 24, 70
  stencil 25
  stripping 12, 22
  traditional 26
  trays 22
  water-based 26
painting 13–14
palettes 22
paper, tracing 26
pediments 14–15
peel and crackle medium 19, 30,
49, 52, 76
pens
  metallic 20
  permanent ink 22
pigments 22
  mixing 32
primer paint 23

rabbit skin glue 23, 66
radiator roller 23
raffia 100
rag rolling 82, 90
rollers, radiator 23

sales
  auctions 10–11
  car boot 10
  garage 9–10
sanding 12
  sandpapers 24
  sealer 23
  wet and dry sandpaper 27
scalpels 24
scumble glaze 26

shops
  charity 11
  junk 9
softening brushes 24
sponges, sea 24
spray mount 24
spray paint 24, 70
stamps 25
stars 44
stencils
  brushes 25
  film 23
  on glass 72
  making 61
  mirrors 82–3
  paint 25
  using 14, 30, 62–3, 90–1
stippling
  brushes 25
  effects 88
stripping 12
  paint strippers 22

tack cloth 26
tape, low tack 21
tracing
  designs 49
  paper 26
transparent mediums 14

varnishes
  acrylic 17
  acrylic glaze 17, 63
  crackle 19
  oil-based 22
  removers 26
  spray 70
  varnishing 36, 95, 104
verdigris effects 39–41

water-based paint 26
wax finish 32, 50, 53, 57, 77
  liming wax 21, 86
wet and dry paper 27
white spirit 27
wire wool 27
wood fillers 27
woodworm 12